Seek the truth.

Huge Arch Press

3119 Rendale Avenue

Richmond, VA 23221-3917

ISBN 1-59801-229-0

Library of Congress Control Number: 2005920329

SIX SECRETS OF SALES MAGNETS

Proven & Powerful Ways To
***Attract** More Sales*

Laura Posey
Will Turner

Read What Others Are Saying About This Book

"Simply the best book on sales and business you will read this year—guaranteed to make a difference in your life."

Ben Meredith
President, B & B Consulting Services, Inc.

"A real pragmatic approach and advice to move yourself from 'average' to 'top' of the game. A smooth read all the way through! I highly recommend it for both sales and marketing folks who are starting out in their career, in a rut, or worse, losing their edge. At the heart, this book is about how to turn 'pushing' yourself on customers into 'attracting' customers to you! As a Chinese proverb reminds us: 'The person that says it cannot be done should not interrupt the person doing it!' This book tells you how to do it!"

Dave Allison
Director, Worldwide Software Sales
& Marketing Strategy, IBM

"When reading this book, I was struck with new, easily applied ways to improve my skills and sales. I've passed this along to each member of our sales team as required reading."

Bill Zadeits
VP & Group Publisher, Cherokee Publishing

"Down with sales techniques, up with sales professionalism. *Six Secrets of Sales Magnets* is all about sales professionalism at the highest level."

Steve Roberts
President,
Carolina Outdoor Lighting Professionals, Inc.

"After reading this book, I can strongly attest to the power and the simple wisdom that Turner and Posey espouse that can help transform an average performer to a super success in business. I can personally profess to the results one can achieve through putting the principles in this book into practice."

Gus Iurillo
Entrepreneur's Source, Consultant of the Year 2004

"Understanding Sales Magnetism has forever changed how I approach my sales initiatives. Now, I choose my clients instead of chasing them."

Alan Hilyer
WSI Internet Consulting and Education

"You have distilled in one small tome what sales trainers have been attempting to write over decades and millions of pages. The basic concept of Bull's Eye Marketing is so simple that it apparently escaped notice by everyone else. It is one of those 'whack your forehead' ideas. Great stuff. If every sales manager gave this book to every new sales hire on their first day, I wouldn't dread answering the phone anymore."

Jim Belfield
Chief Marketing Officer, Colonial Farm Credit

"If you want to become a real 'partner' with your clients, *Six Secrets of Sales Magnets* clearly shows you how you can become indispensable to them, while reaping the rewards of the relationships for yourself!"

Byron Day
The Planning Group

"Will and Laura have provided me the tools to escape from 'Vendorville,' where I have been held, to reside among my clients, who welcome me as someone who values truth in the relationship above all things.

As a business owner who must wear many hats, including sales, I don't have the luxury of wasting my time (nor prospective clients'). Becoming a 'Sales Magnet' allows me to focus my time with people who are the right fit for me and my firm; my clients see me not only as an advisor, but an advocate and a resource. They know that my primary goal is to help them with their business. Read the book. Better yet, live the book!"

Jay B. Cowan
Principle, Cowan Kouri & White Financial Services

"I have read so many books on how to make the sale and the tricks and myths of selling. I wanted something that was different that put a new perspective on what sales and relationships are all about. *Six Secrets of Sales Magnets* did that. It's not about the sale, it's about the relationships you build and the value you add to those relationships."

Matthew Archer
Financial Advisor, Strategic Investments Group

"Awesome book! One of my favorite sayings is 'It has been said that there is little difference between people. It is <u>that</u> difference that makes <u>ALL</u> the difference.' This book explains that difference. Thank you Laura and Will!"

Oie Osterkamp
Vice-President, GetitQuick.com

"The secret is out!! In their book, *Six Secrets of Sales Magnets,* Laura Posey and Will Turner uncover the best practices to sales success in a format that is topical, relatable and relevant to all. A must read for anyone in sales aspiring to be at the top of their field!"

Michael Guld
Author of *The Million Dollar Media Rep.*

"For years, I looked for the next 'trick' to close a deal. With Sales Magnetism, it's very easy, I just need to get to the truth and see if the prospect is in fact a good fit. I don't need to use any closing techniques like the 'assumptive close' or ask a bunch of loaded questions. I just need to ask good questions to see if we are a good fit for each other. It is such a relief and I find that my clients appreciate it so much more."

Ernie Rogers
Auctioneer, The Counts Realty & Auction Group

"Sales Magnetism has changed my life. I spend time getting to know my customer, rather than getting the sale. My sales success has increased dramatically because I've learned to 'W.A.I.T.' This book is packed with infinite wisdom."

Sandra Sylvester
President/CEO, Superior Global Solutions, Inc.

Is This Book for You?

We understand you have lots of options for improving your sales skills. A search on Google for "sales books" alone yields a staggering 14,300,000 entries. While each entry does not represent a different book, the reality is your choices are abundant. So, should you invest your hard-earned money and scarce time on this one? We think that is a very good question to which you deserve a very good answer.

We are Laura Posey and Will Turner, founders of Dancing Elephants Achievement Group, a sales training company. We are seasoned salespeople who have been in the selling trenches for the last two decades. As salespeople, we have learned from our successes, as well as our failures. As sales managers, we have learned from the successes and failures of our sales teams. And as sales trainers, we have learned from the successes and failures of our clients. We want to save you from making many of the same mistakes that are all too common in the world of selling. These are mistakes that you have been taught as the "right" way to sell.

We have found that most salespeople have to get rid of some bad sales habits. Often these bad habits are the result of old selling techniques that no longer work, because selling today is not what it used to be. In the Star Wars® movie, THE EMPIRE STRIKES BACK, Yoda admonishes Luke that, to become great, he must "unlearn what he has learned." YODA, THE EMPIRE STRIKES BACK (Lucasfilm, Ltd. 1980). While most of us do not have to "unlearn" everything we know about sales, we do have to make some mental shifts. For some, these shifts are major. For others, it simply means massaging what they already know and do.

When talking to salespeople, we found that most have been exposed to some form of consultative sales approach. Whether they learned from a book, tapes, training programs or their boss; most salespeople today identify themselves as consultative salespeople. In other words, they espouse wanting to understand their customers so they can help them find the "right" solution to their problems. We took the popular consultative sales process, put it under a microscope and challenged the conventional wisdom. We found that while the basic premise is good, it falls short of delivering the best long-term results.

We also studied salespeople and made some interesting discoveries. While most salespeople do many things right, they are equally guilty of doing many things wrong. In many cases, salespeople exert pressure. Sometimes it is overt and sometimes it is subtle, but it is never good. Salespeople also get stuck in other traps like talking too much, not asking the right questions and not being focused. Most tend to wing it, and many are not able to create enough value in their relationships. Even more telling is that most salespeople do not even realize they are doing anything wrong. They just know they are not as successful as they want to be.

In our quest for a better "sales" mousetrap, we developed a program called Sales Magnetism. We have used our Sales Magnetism approach to train countless salespeople and the results have been astonishing. Our average client increases sales 56% in the first year of working with us. We take results very seriously, and we think you should too.

To determine if this book is right for you, take the following quiz:

1. I realize my full sales potential every week and consistently exceed my sales goals
   ☐ YES   ☐ NO

2. I successfully close 75% or more of my prospects.
   ☐ YES   ☐ NO

3. I have peer-to-peer relationships with all of my clients and I am not treated like just another vendor.
   ☐ YES   ☐ NO

4. I never use closing techniques to get the business.
   ☐ YES   ☐ NO

5. At least 50% of my business comes from repeat business and/or referrals.
   ☐ YES   ☐ NO

6. I never misrepresent the truth or tell "little white lies" to my clients or prospects.
   ☐ YES   ☐ NO

7. I am sought out and treated as a trusted advisor.
   ☐ YES   ☐ NO

8. I attract 20% or more of my business because of my reputation as an expert in my field.
   ☐ YES   ☐ NO

9. I have at least five referral sources who consistently send me five or more qualified referrals per year that turn into clients.
   ☐ YES   ☐ NO

10. I hold myself 100% responsible for my results every week.
    ☐ YES   ☐ NO

If you answered "NO" to any of the above statements, you will probably find this book eye-opening, and at times, even a little radical. You cannot expect to do the same old things and get amazing results. Be warned now, however, that you will not find quick fixes or flashy techniques in this book. Those simply do not work. Instead, you will find six ways to distinguish yourself and become the best at what you do.

The bottom-line is that you will get out of this book what you are willing to put into practice by applying the lessons you will learn. Do you want to be the top salesperson for your office, your company or your industry? Do you feel you have room to improve? More importantly, do you want to improve? If you are open to change and ready to embrace new ideas, you will get real value in the pages that follow. Enjoy your journey!

Dedication

Thanks to everyone who has made this book possible—
our friends, families and colleagues who believed in
us and made our efforts fun and rewarding. Special
thanks to Jeanne, Terry, Jackie, Mike, Ellen, Jerry and
Crandall; all of whom bless us with their love and
support. Thanks to the staff at Stir Crazy on
MacArthur Avenue, definitely the best coffee shop in
Richmond, Virginia to write and edit a book.

Also, thanks to Tim Moore, our esteemed
colleague in Cary, North Carolina. Tim's contributions helped shape and improve this book. His
wisdom and sales experience are real assets to
Dancing Elephants Achievement Group.

Most of all, this book is dedicated to the
thousands of salespeople whom we have had the
pleasure of working with and knowing. You have all
taught us and we value your many insights and your
dedication to your profession. You continue to make
our journey rich and meaningful.

Be Magnetic,

Laura & Will

Table of Contents

(I N T R O D U C T I O N)

No More Plaid Jackets!

In 1978, television audiences were introduced to a slick-talking, polyester-wearing salesman named Herb Tarlek. Herb was the salesman for WKRP in Cincinnati. And it is the image of Herb, and others like him, who fit our stereotype of the pushy, unrelenting salesperson.

Back in the '70's, salespeople like Herb would try to manipulate and charm their buyers. Herb was quite the charmer, even though the sincerity of his remarks was usually suspect. Herb thought a little flattery, however insincere or sexist, was a good thing. And in his day, it worked – from time to time.

Back then salespeople like Herb were often the only game in town. The competition certainly was not global like it is today, so it was easier to sell by being a smooth talker. Buyers needed products and services and they had limited options. They did not have the Internet to do research and they did not have global communications to find other sellers.

They also were not as jaded as they are today, having been promised things by salespeople like Herb that never quite lived up to all the sales hype.

Fast forward to the present. Most of us today laugh at the image of Herb and others like him. We think we are different and better. And thankfully, we are for the most part. We are not as pushy; but have we really removed all the slick sales techniques and pressure from our words and actions? We are not so insincere, but do we still say things we think the prospect wants to hear even though they may not be 100% true? We may have shed our plaid jackets, yet our image as salespeople, as a whole, is still tarnished.

The truth is most salespeople have changed some, but there are parts of Herb that are still with us. It is not surprising when you think about it. Many of us have been taught to say whatever is necessary in order to make the sale. We have been taught to advance the sale even when it may not be in the prospect's best interest. We have been taught the ABCs of sales—Always Be Closing. We have been taught that sales is a numbers game, so it is alright that we only close 20% to 30% of our prospects. And we have even been taught to disguise the seamier side of selling by expressing empathy and using a more consultative, problem-solving approach with our prospects.

In other words, we have been taught to act differently than Herb on the surface, but the transformation has not always been complete below the surface. The purpose of this book is to look beyond the outer changes and get down to the core reasons why most salespeople are just average. More importantly, this book is intended to help you move from average to good to great.

We want to help you recognize some of the things that may be holding you back. Are your actions and words congruent with the salesperson you want to be? Do you sell with complete integrity and honesty, or are there times when you stretch things a bit? Are you actively sought out as a resource by your prospects and clients or do you have to call them? Do you close 75% or more of your prospects without resorting to manipulative closing techniques or do you find yourself still "selling" sometimes?

Are you the top salesperson in your company making the money that you want to make or are you stuck in the middle of the pack? Do you work 40 hours a week and live the life you dream of or do you work really hard just to make ends meet? Maybe you are somewhere in-between.

To be the best in sales, you cannot act like Herb; that is a given. But, you also cannot be as you were five years, three years or even a year ago. Times have changed and you must also if you want to get ahead. If you do not change and evolve, you may find yourself facing the same fate as Herb and his plaid jacket.

Are you AVERAGE, GOOD or GREAT?

$$\boxed{\text{C H A P T E R} \cdot \text{1}}$$

What Type of Salesperson Are You?

If you have ever been in sales or know anyone who has, you know that salespeople come in all shapes and sizes. They are often as different on the inside as they are on the outside. There are some huge differences not only in the way salespeople work but in the results they get.

Some salespeople work like dogs while others make it look effortless and fun. Ironically, the ones who make it look effortless and fun earn tons of money while the ones who work the hardest are often struggling financially. How can that be? What is the difference between these salespeople? Is the successful group just born to be in sales? Is the struggling group just not cut out for the profession?

These questions are perplexing; even bothersome. What is the difference between salespeople and their results? How do some people get rich in sales, maintain their integrity, earn the respect of their clients and peers and live lives that others only dream of? Why are some salespeople struggling just to make ends meet?

▶ The Different Types Of Salespeople

There are four types of salespeople. The first group is the Short-Timers. This group consists of people who try sales, but do not last in the field for more than a few years. They either give up or are fired because they lack the discipline or the necessary skills to eke out a comfortable living. We will not be spending any time on them.

The remaining salespeople fall into three general categories—Average, Professional and Magnetic. These categories correspond to average, good and great. The world is full of Average salespeople. They jump or fall into sales and they make a decent living, but they struggle to take their performance to the next level. While they would like to make more money, they find themselves stuck in the land of status quo or are lulled into a state of complacency.

Average salespeople simply fall short. Some fall short from lack of effort, others work very hard but lack the know-how or necessary skills. Either way, they remain stuck in Average.

The next category is Professional salespeople. They have figured out what Average salespeople have not. They perform at a more productive level and they generally feel good about their careers and their lives.

The final category is made up of Magnetic salespeople. These men and women have risen to the top of their fields. They are great salespeople who are highly respected and sought out by others.

Magnetic salespeople represent only about 5% of all salespeople. But it doesn't have to be that way. In this book, you will learn the differences between the three types of salespeople and how you can progress from Average or Professional to Magnetic.

This transition is an evolution. You will not wake up to the life that you dream of by wishing it was so. You can, however, wake up and start doing the things you need to do to get there. The length of your personal journey depends upon your starting point and your ability to embrace change.

If you are an Average salesperson, the evolution to a Sales Magnet will take longer than if you are starting out as a Professional. In fact, Average salespeople have to make some drastic changes to reach Professional status. Professionals, on the other hand, need to make important changes to become Magnets, but those changes are much more subtle.

▶ A Face To Go With The Label

We would like to introduce you to a few salespeople we know. One is Average, one is Professional and one is Magnetic. You will find out how they sell and why their lives are so different. Maybe you will even recognize some things about yourself in them.

The Average Salesperson

Meet Alex. Alex is a typical Average salesperson. He sells phone systems for a locally-owned company in his hometown. He has been in sales for about 10 years and with his current company for two years. Alex, his wife and their two kids live in a 1980's neighborhood in the house they bought when they were first married six years ago. Alex's wife Judy is a teacher and their kids go to the public elementary school where she teaches. Alex and Judy both work hard. It is not unusual for Alex to put in 50 to 60 hours per week. On top of her busy teaching day, Judy assumes most of the childcare responsibilities because Alex works longer days than she does.

Alex spends his days selling. He usually makes about 20 to 30 cold calls per day, does several drop-ins and has an appointment or two. He spends the rest of his time following up on closed deals, providing customer service and handling the fires that come up. No matter how hard he works, though, he just cannot seem to get to where he wants to be. He is not doing badly; he has made about $60,000 to $65,000 for each of the last three years, which is better than many of his friends have done. One year he even made $75,000 when he closed a big deal at a new factory in town. He wonders, though, why he cannot seem to break through his plateau and get to the six-figure income others seem to be making.

Alex's life hasn't changed much in the last three or four years. He is a little savvier and has a few more battle scars to show off, but he still goes about his business the same old way. He makes cold calls, he works harder than he thinks he should, and he is still not making the money he was promised when he moved to the new company. He believes he is a good salesman, but he wonders why he does not get the things he wants more often.

The Professional Salesperson

Then there is Paula. Paula is a Professional salesperson. She works for a large investment company and sells life insurance and other financial products in the same town Alex lives in. She has been in sales for about 10 years and is with her second employer since graduating from college. Paula is married and has a young son. Her husband Ted writes for the local newspaper. Paula and her family live in a stately brick Colonial built in the 1930's. The house has been completely renovated and Paula and Ted love the close-knit neighborhood. They have a good life and really look forward to their vacations and weekend get-aways. They alternate between trips to Sanibel Island, Florida and Cape Cod, Massachusetts.

Paula, like Alex, works hard each day. She spends about 50 hours a week at work, spreading her time between cold calling, networking activities, seeing prospects and doing paperwork. She spends a few nights a week and about two weekends a month at clients' homes, presenting and selling. She does not mind the long hours but she would like to be at home with her family more often in the evening. Paula rationalizes the night work by thinking about the six-figure income she earns. Last year, she made $115,000. She reminds herself that not everyone can make that kind of money and she is thankful for what she has. She is always afraid that if she slows down, she might lose some business and her income will drop.

Paula has an easier work life than some. Her closing ratio is one of the highest in her office and she is frequently excused from some of the rules and regulations imposed on lesser producers by her boss. All in all, she lives a good life. She has enough money to do many of the things she wants and just enough time to enjoy many of them. She worries about saving for college and retirement and she watches her budget closely, but she and her family do not want for much.

The Magnetic Salesperson

Mark is a Magnetic salesperson, and what a life he has. He has been selling printing for the last four years and sold advertising for six years before that. Mark, his wife Maria, and their three children live in a beautiful new neighborhood in the suburbs. They just bought their dream house a year ago and are busy decorating and filling it with things they love.

Maria works in the home and cares for the children. They attend private school, freeing up Maria to volunteer her spare time with a couple local charities. Mark and his family love their home but look forward to vacation time too. Each year they plan a two-week vacation to a different country and then take smaller trips throughout the year. Mark also indulges his love of fishing. He frequently takes three-day weekends to go out on the river in search of the big catch.

Mark is a hard worker, but he has figured out how to work smartly, too. He works 40–45 hours per week and never misses an important family event. He made $230,000 last year and has an assistant who handles administrative and operational tasks for him so he can focus on what he does best—building relationships. He never has to cold call and in fact, prospects often call him first. He spends his days meeting with new people and racking up sales.

He always seems at ease and never worries where his next paycheck is coming from or how much commission he has earned. Everyone in his company looks up to him and the other salespeople want to emulate him if they could only figure out how. When asked his secret, he does not have a concise answer. To him selling has become as natural as breathing.

Mark really is living the good life. He has the respect of his clients and peers, time to spend on his hobbies and family and enough income to do what he chooses. He is in control of his income and can earn more at will so that nothing is financially out of his reach. To other salespeople he seems to be a born salesperson, lucky or both.

▶ The Terminology

So why are some salespeople Average like Alex, some Professional like Paula and others Magnetic like Mark? It has nothing to do with luck or birth. It has to do with their attitudes and their behaviors. That is it. It is what they think and do that separates them. Interestingly, the differences in their thinking and actions are quite small compared to the outcomes they experience.

The Average

Average salespeople are mediocre. If they were in school, they would get a "C" for their efforts. They make a decent but not a great living, and they represent most of the salespeople in the world. From our research, we estimate that approximately 75% of all salespeople fall in the Average range.

Since Average salespeople represent most salespeople, when we think of salespeople in general we usually think of the Average. So what comes to mind when you think of the word "salesperson?" Pushy, manipulative, tricky, money-hungry or flashy?

Salespeople in our culture are people we are taught to avoid, lie to and try to get the best of. Even Merriam-Webster® gets in on the action. Here are the dictionary's first seven definitions of "sell":

1: to deliver or give up in violation of duty, trust, or loyalty: **<u>BETRAY</u>**—often used with *out*

2a(1): to give up (property) to another for something of value (as money) **(2):** to offer for sale **b:** to give up in return for something else especially foolishly or dishonorably <*sold* his birthright for a mess of pottage> **c:** to exact a price for <*sold* their lives dearly>

3a: to deliver into slavery for money **b:** to give into the power of another <*sold* his soul to the devil> **c:** to deliver the personal services of for money

4: to dispose of or manage for profit instead of in accordance with conscience, justice, or duty <*sold* their votes>

5a: to develop a belief in the truth, value, or desirability of: gain acceptance for <trying to *sell* a program to the Congress> **b:** to persuade or influence to a course of action or to the acceptance of something <*sell* children on reading>

6: to impose on: **<u>CHEAT</u>**

7a: to cause or promote the sale of <using television advertising to sell cereal> **b:** to make or attempt to make sales to **c:** to influence or induce to make a purchase

It is not until definition 5b that there is anything positive stated about selling! Is it any wonder salespeople are looked at with such disdain? Is there anything in those definitions that you would want to be known for?

The Professional

While Professional salespeople represent the next step up in the sales hierarchy, they are worlds away from the Average. As 20% of all salespeople, they have taken their skills and abilities to the next level. They are good at what they do and are well-respected. In fact, they are offended by the notion that Average salespeople have tarnished their good profession.

What comes to mind when you think about the word "professional?" Well-educated, well-dressed, intelligent, caring, committed and dedicated? You get the picture. Professionals are people we look up to and to whom we listen and turn to for advice and counsel. Often we consider such occupations as doctors, lawyers, and accountants as "professions." Other occupations, sales included, fall into the categories of "career" or "job."

It is not just our perceptions that put professionals at a different level. Merriam-Webster® defines "professional" as:

> **1:** characterized by or conforming to the *technical or ethical standards* of a <u>profession</u> **2:** exhibiting *a courteous, conscientious, and generally businesslike* manner in the workplace

and "profession" as:

> **1a:** a calling requiring *specialized knowledge* and

often long and intensive academic preparation **b:** a principal calling, vocation, or employment."

Every single definition of professional is positive and brings up images of honesty, conviction and dedication.

The Magnet

Magnetic salespeople represent the top 5% of all salespeople. They do many of the things Professional salespeople do, but they do them a little better. The divide between Magnetic and Professional is not that wide; the differences are actually subtle, yet very meaningful. People want to do business with Magnets, because they are the best at what they do.

Magnets are the cream of the crop. They have reached a level of sales competence where everything comes naturally. They are trusted advisors to their clients and they are sought out as experts by prospects.

According to the Merriam-Webster® dictionary, Magnetic means "possessing an extraordinary power or ability to attract." And that's exactly what Magnetic salespeople do; they attract business. Others are drawn to them and want to work with them because of their reputation, character and expertise.

Magnetic salespeople attract others because they do not act like other salespeople. They never exert sales pressure, because that repels prospects away. Instead, these top performers draw others closer. It is easy for them. Magnetic salespeople put others first and build trusting relationships. They naturally earn the respect and loyalty of all the people with whom they interact.

Three Types of Salespeople
Key Differences at a Glance

	AVERAGE	PROFESSIONAL	MAGNETIC
Annual income	$35,000 – $70,000	$75,000 – $125,000	$150,000 +
Hours worked per week	50 – 70	45 – 60	40 – 45
Closing ratio	20% – 30%	40% – 60%	70% +
Rank among peers	Bottom 75%	Top 20%	Top 5%

(C H A P T E R • 2)

Become an Expert

▶ Alex—The Average Salesperson

It is Sunday evening and as the sun begins to set and the weekend comes to a close, Alex begins to get a knot in his stomach. His mind has been free from the rigors of his sales job all weekend, but now as he puts his children to bed and starts to think about Monday morning, he becomes anxious. Even his wife notices the change in his mood.

Alex thinks of all the things he has to do at work this week. He has some fires to put out. He cannot help thinking of the voice mail he got from Sue Taylor on Friday afternoon. She is a new client and she did not sound happy. "It is always something," Alex thinks.

On top of that, he is behind on his prospecting calls. "Who will I call this week? It is always a struggle to come up with more people to call," Alex laments. As Alex gets into bed and drifts off to sleep he tells himself, "There's got to be a better way." Alex's sleep is restless. He begrudgingly rolls out of bed at 6:00 a.m. Monday morning so he can get an early start to his day.

Alex arrives at the office and grabs a cup of coffee. At 7:25 a.m., he sits down at his desk to plan his weekly call activity. "I'm not in the mood for this today," thinks Alex, "Who am I going to call this week?" Cold calling is one of Alex's least favorite activities, but he knows it is a necessary evil.

Alex's sales manager, Jerry, is always harping on the number of calls Alex and his co-workers need to make. The magic number is 100 a week. It seems like an arbitrary number to Alex, but he knows that he has to play the game.

Jerry was a very successful salesperson for the company before being promoted to Sales Manager about 12 years ago. He was a cold calling machine in his day. Of course Alex and the rest of the sales team like to joke that Jerry was "king" back in the rotary phone days before caller ID and administrative assistants from hell. At the end of their Tuesday morning sales meetings, Jerry always sends his troops back to their desks with the same advice, "It's a numbers game, so start dialing the numbers!"

After 10 minutes sorting through some papers on his desk, Alex knows that he has to buckle down. "I've got to suck it up and get going on this. These calls aren't going to make themselves," Alex grumbles. "I wonder who I should call? Companies who are moving soon or expanding are great candidates. I did doctors last week because my friend said his doctor's office was growing. But how does anyone ever get in to see doctors? Maybe lawyers will be easier. They are always adding partners and stuff – they ought to be a good category." Alex grabs his local Chamber of Commerce directory and looks up attorneys, finding just 20 listed. "Great, I need at least 100, plus the ones I'm behind from last week. Maybe I can look in the phone book and pull names from the ads. I'll bet there are tons in there."

As he flips through the 30 pages of attorneys listed in the phone book Alex thinks, "This is crazy, there must be hundreds of law firms in here! How am I going to decide which ones are best? I don't want to waste my time on the little ones, but how can I tell? It looks like some of them list themselves individually as well as with their firms. Maybe lawyers aren't such a good idea. Let's look up accountants and see what's there. They're similar to lawyers."

Forty-five minutes later, Alex has finally settled on architects as this week's target market. He found a list online of the local members of the Architect's Association and there were 114 of them listed, plenty to make his weekly cold call quota. "Now I just have to make the calls," sighs Alex. "I wish they'd just hire someone to do this for me. What a waste of my skills. I should be closing, not prospecting."

▶ Paula — The Professional Salesperson

Paula is planning her prospecting activities for the week as well. "Let's see who's in the paper this week. There are always some good leads in the *People in Business* section," thinks Paula. She leafs through the local newspaper and she writes down the names of people who look like good prospects.

Paula has found that small business owners are

great prospects for her. Her local paper lists new business licenses, as well as general announcements about local business expansions and changes. "Wow, it looks like a good week. I've got over 20 names already!" Paula thinks excitedly "This could be a big week."

After picking out her names to call for the week, Paula checks her calendar to see what else she has going on. She already has three appointments scheduled for the week from referrals and has also set a meeting with her strategic alliance partners.

Two years ago, Paula gathered together a small group of professionals to form a strategic alliance. Her group includes an accountant, an attorney and a health insurance provider. They share information and refer each other business. They jokingly refer to themselves as The Four Amigos, since they really value their friendships, as well as their professional affiliation. They all target small business owners and each has existing clients they refer to each other. They meet twice a month to exchange information on new clients and prospects and strategize how they can introduce their new contacts to the others in the alliance. Paula gets a lot of good business from The Four Amigos and her clients benefit from the referrals she gives them from the group as well.

"I have enough names to get three or four more appointments," muses Paula, "but I'd like a few more. I guess I'd better make room in my schedule to call some clients this week. If I call 10 clients, I'll get at least one good referral or a new sale. Besides, I promised I'd check in on them quarterly when I wrote their policies and I can't afford to let my reputation slip."

"It's going to be another good week," thinks Paula as she puts her new prospects in her calendar to call.

▶ Mark—The Magnetic Salesperson

"Good morning, this is Mark," he answers after picking up the ringing phone.

"Hi, Mark, it's Tony from Whitlow and Besosa." Mark immediately recognizes Tony as a partner for one of his client firms.

"Hi Tony, what can I do for you this morning?"

"Mark, I'm wondering if you can do me a favor. As you know, our Marketing Manager, Cindy left last month and we've been searching for her replacement. Well, we've finally found someone and she started this week. Her name is Erika Brandt. Erika is new to the field but we think she's got great potential. I know you're really involved in the Legal Marketing Association and I was wondering if you could take her to a meeting and introduce her to some people?"

"Congratulations on finding someone. Of course, I'd be happy to show Erika around and make sure she knows who's who. I'll come by this week to introduce myself and invite her personally to the meeting at the end of the month. How's that?" asks Mark.

"That's perfect. Can you do me one more favor Mark? Cindy said you know more about our marketing and direct mail campaigns than anyone around here. Could you take Erika to lunch, on me of course, and get her up to speed? Cindy left her some good notes, but it would really help to have your insights."

"I'd love to have lunch with Erika. It will give us a chance to get to know each other, and it will make it easier for me to connect her to the right people. I've got an opening next Thursday. Do you think that will work in Erika's calendar?"

"I'll make it her first official appointment. Thanks, Mark. I knew I could count on you."

After hanging up, Mark smiles, thinking about his upcoming lunch. Tony's firm has always been a good client and it feels good to be helping them out.

"Time to start prospecting for the week," thinks Mark as he gets out his attendee list from the presentation he made on Friday. Mark was the speaker at a Legal Marketing Association event last week and it is time to plan his follow up calls to the 30 attendees. Many of them are already his clients, but there are 14 that are not. Mark is finishing up the thank you notes and some supplementary information to send and then he'll schedule his follow up calls. Just as he's setting aside the last note, the phone rings again.

"Hi Mark, this is Erika from Whitlow and Besosa. Tony just gave me your name and number and said you were the person I needed to talk to."

Secret #1

Average Salespeople **Are Generalists**
Professional Salespeople **Are Specialists**
Magnetic Salespeople **Are Experts**

▶ Average Salespeople Are Generalists

Like other Average salespeople, Alex is your classic generalist. His clients cover the whole gamut of industries, from law to manufacturing to insurance. He knows that most of his clients buy when they are getting ready to make a major change or expansion but beyond that he has no idea what they have in common, if anything. He chooses his target for the week or for the month based on how easy it is to get a list to call. He hopes he gets an industry that moves and changes frequently, but it always seems like it is a matter of luck and good timing.

His prospecting could best be described as the shotgun approach. He fires at anything that looks like it might be a prospect. Alex was taught that this wide-angle approach is best because he never misses a chance to sell something. His philosophy, which he learned from his boss, is that "sales is a numbers game." If he makes enough calls, regardless of to whom, he will get some sales and hit his quota. He dials and dials. While Alex does not enjoy cold calling, he has learned to tolerate it.

The shotgun approach to prospecting is the demise of many Average salespeople. Because they are constantly shifting their focus to different markets or products and services, they never build up any real traction or become known for anything. They find themselves stuck in a sales rut, cold calling and dropping in on prospects, usually with no research or understanding of whether the person they are trying to reach is a good match for them or not. Even when they network, they fail to position themselves to be remembered. They waste time and energy hoping to be at the right place at the right time.

Like other Average salespeople, Alex is convinced that enough calls will yield the results he wants. What Alex does not realize about his numbers game is that the odds are stacked against him. His cold calling produces a 10% appointment ratio and a 2% closing ratio. That means he has to dial 10 numbers to get an appointment and 50 numbers to eventually get a sale. With all the other things he does, 50 calls take about two days to complete, so he only makes a sale every week or two. No wonder his job is so hard.

▶ Professional Salespeople Are Specialists

As a Professional salesperson, Paula's approach to prospecting is more focused. Paula has decided she can make a very good living working with small business owners and she only markets to them. She has spent time creating strategic alliances with other like-minded professionals and her strategy is paying off. She receives enough referrals to have a strong sales foundation, but she cannot meet her income goals by referrals and repeat clients alone.

In addition to the referrals she gets from The Four Amigos and her clients, Paula rounds out her prospecting activities with networking and old-fashioned cold calling. Luckily for her, Paula finds that she is cold calling less with each passing year in the business. Paula spends her time marketing herself to small business owners and making sure her referral sources know she specializes in that market.

Like other Professional salespeople, Paula really understands the value of specialization. She has analyzed her sales process and found that by specializing and narrowing her focus, she has become better compensated and more effective. She enjoys what she does now more than when she was just starting out and was lacking her current clarity.

Compare this strategy of specialization to other fields. Think about doctors. The most highly compensated doctors are not the general practitioners who work on the entire human body. The most compensated are specialists who treat only the brain, the heart, wrists or knees. The more specialized someone is, the more we pay her, the harder she is to get in to see and the more control she has over the people she works with.

Attorneys are more highly compensated when they specialize in one area of law like real estate, bankruptcy, tax or employment law. Accountants are more highly compensated when they deal with a particular industry like construction or banking. Psychiatrists make the big bucks when they concentrate on particular illnesses such as depression or schizophrenia.

Professionals have figured out that specialization gives them much more credibility than generalization.

The reason the heart surgeon does not work on elbows is that he knows that the time he spends researching elbows and learning the surgical techniques will take away from the time he has to become a better heart surgeon. Not only that, but his billing for the elbow work, as a generalist, is far less than his billing for heart surgery, as a specialist. Even if he does not have a heart patient in his office, his time is better spent looking for more heart patients or studying heart surgery than it is treating a sore elbow.

▶ Magnetic Salespeople Are Experts

The difference between Mark and Paula is that Mark has taken his specialization to the level of expertise. Like other experts, Mark has established himself as the printing resource that people in his chosen market—law firms—want to talk to. Salespeople who become experts are Magnets because others are attracted to them.

People want to do business with the best, and they are willing to pay the price to obtain the best. Think about it. If you need heart surgery, do you look up someone in the Yellow Pages? Of course not. You seek referrals from people you know and trust. You do some additional research, if necessary, to find the best. Price is not even in the equation.

Mark's reputation as an expert has allowed him to forgo traditional prospecting activities. He has not made a cold call in years.

Mark's ascent to the status of expert took years. He started by concentrating only on printing sales to law firms. In other words, he became a specialist, much the same way that Paula has. But over time, he has taken it to the top level.

To build his expertise, he focused on one market and concentrated on learning everything he could about it. Mark chose to focus on law firms and the area of legal marketing. Mark had been a political science major in college. He had thought about law school, but he opted for a focus in Marketing and a MBA in graduate school instead. Given his background, the idea of the legal field was interesting to him.

In addition, Mark already had a few law firm clients. He realized that they had ongoing printing and marketing needs and that they were concerned about projecting a professional image. That translated into higher-end printing jobs – ones that needed to be well-thought out and designed. They had to be more strategic. Consequently, he could add more value with his advice and insights and make more money at the same time. Mark knows his focus on selling higher-end printing jobs beats pounding the pavement to sell low-margin orders of business cards and letterhead, which his company also produces.

In choosing a market to focus on, Mark also knew that the legal marketing field was going through some transitions upon which he could capitalize. Law firms were shifting away from a more staid and traditional approach where they relied solely on word-of-mouth and repeat business to maintain their revenue stream. They were finding that in order to be competitive they had to introduce more aggressive marketing and practice development strategies. Mark saw the opportunities clearly and took action. As a Magnetic salesperson, Mark knew that a narrow and singular focus on one market—a Bull's Eye Market—would yield the biggest results in the long-term.

Bull's Eye Marketing

You are probably familiar with the concept of niche or target marketing. It simply means that you narrow your focus to those markets that are most likely to have a need for your products or services. Bull's Eye Marketing is similar; it just takes niche marketing and drills down a little deeper.

With Bull's Eye Marketing, you choose to specialize in one area. You can specialize by the market you serve, the product/service you offer or both. Choosing a singular focus will streamline your efforts and energy and lead to better results. With experience, your chosen area of specialization will become your area of expertise. When that happens, you will attract significantly more business as a Sales Magnet.

Like other Sales Magnets, Mark knew he had to increase his knowledge and visibility in his Bull's Eye Market. He began sponsoring the local Bar Association meetings. Later he became an associate member. He studied the field, doing research and reading everything he could on the subject. Magnetic salespeople know that building their knowledge with a particular Bull's Eye Market, defined by industry or job function, will enhance their expertise and increase their credibility with their chosen prospects.

Mark continues to build his knowledge base so he can remain on the front end of the industry's learning curve. He reads the latest articles in the national trade magazines and actively engages in staying abreast of trends and issues that affect his prospects. Now, he is sought out as a speaker by the local law school and attends every legal marketing meeting and conference he can. He has developed close relationships not only with lawyers, but more importantly, with the legal marketing associates. He creates seminars and newsletters just for them. He is the expert in legal marketing in the state and everyone knows his name and what he does. That is why he gets calls every week from people seeking his services.

Occasionally Mark gets calls from people in other industries who want his services. He usually politely refers them to someone else in his printing company. Just like the heart surgeon, he realizes that

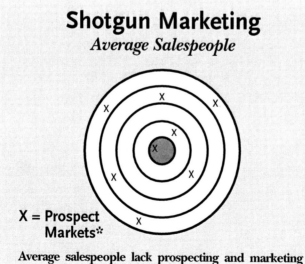

Shotgun Marketing
Average Salespeople

X = Prospect Markets*

Average salespeople lack prospecting and marketing focus. They believe sales is a "numbers game" and use a shotgun approach to marketing and sales.

* Defined by industry or job title.

Niche Marketing
Professional Salespeople

X = Prospect Markets*

Professional salespeople narrow their prospecting and marketing focus to a few key areas. They are less scattered than Average salespeople but not as focused as Magnetic salespeople.

* Defined by industry or job title.

every moment he spends in another industry limits his growth. He is more interested in studying and applying his knowledge so he can gain even greater expertise in his field. The more expertise he has, the more he will get paid. It is a fact that experts are able to charge more than others in their field because they bring more value to the table.

Professional athletes understand the concept of building expertise. Many of them are great athletes, but they get paid to play only one sport. Consequently, they focus all of their time and effort on their sport and becoming an expert in their position. Barry

Bonds gets paid to hit the cover off the ball. Phil Mickelson is a great golfer because he is not trying to be a great baseball player too. Yes, Michael Jordan is a very good golfer, in addition to being an extraordinary basketball player, but when he was in the prime of his professional NBA career, he was never confused over what took priority, practicing his golf swing or practicing his jump shot. Magnetic salespeople do the same thing. They determine where they need to focus their time and energy and what needs to take priority. They do not waste their valuable time trying to be all things to all people.

Bull's Eye Marketing
Magnetic Salespeople

X = Prospect Markets*

Magnetic salespeople narrow their prospecting and marketing focus to a singular area where they develop expertise. They become the best at what they do and refer business to other referral partners and strategic alliances outside their area of expertise.

* Defined by industry or job title.

Summary

To become more Magnetic, you should:

- Narrow your focus and streamline your energy in one area.

- Choose a Bull's Eye Market that represents a group of prospects who are a good match for your goals and your interests.

- Seek quality of prospects over quantity of prospects.

- Become an expert on a product or service, as well as a specific market defined by industry or job title.

- Build your knowledge base by immersing yourself in learning opportunities that relate to better serving your Bull's Eye Market.

- Become involved and contribute to your field.

- Improve your visibility by becoming known and sought after.

CHAPTER • 3

Old MacDonald Had a Farm...

▶ **Alex—The Average Salesperson**

"Hi, Mr. Baldwin, it's Alex from PhoneMax. How are you today?" Alex says, calling his newest client.

"Hi, Alex, I'm fine. How are you doing?" replies Mr. Baldwin.

"I'm great, Mr. Baldwin. I just wanted to call to see how the new phones are working for you. Do you like them?"

"The phones are working great, although it's an adjustment learning all the new features. They really are as good as you said they were though. Thanks for helping us with them."

"I'm glad you like them. As far as the features go, let me know if you need more help on them and I'll send one of our trainers over to give you some lessons. We want you to be satisfied with our service," answers Alex.

"That's good to know. I'll see how it goes this week and get back to you on that."

"I'll look forward to hearing from. Mr. Baldwin," Alex clears his throat, "while I've got you on the phone, may I ask you a question? I know you're satisfied with our service so I was wondering if you know anyone else like yourself that might be interested in our phones. I thought maybe you would know someone else I could talk to about them. Do you?" Alex asks.

"Well, Alex" Mr. Baldwin hesitates, "I'm not sure I know anyone right off the top of my head."

"Maybe you know someone else in manufacturing, like Clanton Enterprises down the street?" replies Alex, somewhat anxiously.

"Sorry Alex, I don't know them. But if I think of someone, I'll be sure to mention you. I've got another call coming in so I've got to run. Thanks again Alex," responds Mr. Baldwin as he hangs up.

"Grrrr, I never get any decent referrals," thinks Alex. "Why don't my customers send me business? He said he liked our work. What's wrong with him?" Alex thinks about his conversations with Mr. Baldwin. "He seems to like me. He even told me that I remind him of his son. Maybe it's these complicated phones or our customer service department."

▶ Paula — The Professional Salesperson

"Ah, Tuesday morning, it's going to be a great day," thinks Paula as she sits down at her desk. As she checks her computer for her task list, she sees it is time to send two birthday cards to clients this week. She also has a note to follow up on a sale from yesterday and needs to schedule annual reviews with four clients.

She grabs her stack of birthday cards and quickly jots a personal note to each recipient. One of them is having a 40th birthday so she adds a special note in the card. She then takes out her thank you notes and jots the following words to a couple she just closed yesterday:

Dear Mr. and Mrs. Bennett,

Thank you so much for allowing me to assist you with your life insurance and financial planning needs. It was a pleasure meeting your family.

I look forward to ensuring your financial security for many years to come. Please feel free to call me if you need anything at all. I'm always at your service.

Best regards,

Paula

"Two things down and one to go. I've just got time to knock out these calls before my next appointment," Paula thinks as she turns to her database for the phone numbers of her clients due for review.

Her first three calls go well and she sets appointments for the following week to meet with her clients. With any luck she'll get a few referrals from them. Her fourth call is a little different. Mr. Mountcastle has been a client for about three years and has been through two annual reviews. He was a tough sell, and he's very picky about his policies.

"It's time for your annual review again, so I was hoping we could schedule something next week. Does that work for you?" Paula says after introducing herself and exchanging some pleasantries.

"Well, Paula, I don't think there's anything I need this year, so maybe we can skip it. I think I have all the insurance I need," replies Mr. Mountcastle, sounding firm.

"Mr. Mountcastle, you know this isn't a time for me to sell you anything, it's just a review to make sure things haven't changed in your life to the extent that we need to alter coverage. Wouldn't you like to be sure that's true?"

"Paula, nothing has changed in the last year for me so I don't think we really need to meet. I really am so busy I don't have the time anyway. I appreciate the call and I'll be sure to call you if anything does change. I've got to run now, but thanks again for the follow up," says Mr. Mountcastle. Paula thanks him, too, and they hang up.

"I hate when that happens. I wonder why some customers do that?" thinks Paula as her good mood from the morning becomes a distant memory.

▶ Mark—The Magnetic Salesperson

"Looks like a great day for golf," Mark smiles as he reviews his calendar for the day. "Just a few details to get out of the way and then it's off to the links."

Mark sits at his desk and checks his task list for the day. It is his day to complete his e-newsletter. Mark has a few articles to finish writing and editing for his monthly publication that goes to all Marketing Directors and assistants in law firms in his database. He has a couple of hours blocked off on his calendar in the morning to make sure everything gets done on time for another edition. Then he will check with his assistant about the event she is coordinating for some clients and their families at a baseball game. After that, it is his regularly scheduled golf game with a client. Each month, Mark golfs with a different client who brings a guest to meet Mark. Mark, in turn, brings someone who could be useful for the client's business.

Once the articles are done, Mark settles in to make a few calls. They typically go like this:

"Hi, Sara, it's Mark. How are you today?"

"Hi, Mark. I'm doing fine, and yourself?"

"You know me, Sara, always top of the world. So, how are things going at the firm?" asks Mark.

"Let me tell you, it's been a zoo around here lately. We have a new client that's larger than any we've ever had and on top of that, Mary, our admin is out on maternity leave. We've got files up to our necks! Everyone has been working late and folks are a bit grumpy right now."

"Wow, that sounds tough. Do you need some extra help, on a temporary basis, while Mary is out?"

"That would be great, but we don't have time to find someone much less get them up to speed when they get here," Sara sighs.

"I've got a friend who owns a legal staffing company and she could probably get you some help by tomorrow if that works for you. Her name is Angie and she's with Alliance Personnel. She's a real dynamo. She has the best pool of talent for legal administrative support, most of whom are paralegals, so I'm sure she could place someone who could jump right in and help you without a lot of hand holding on your part."

"Really? Now, that you mention it, I have heard

Angie's name before. I think Laura over at Pilc and Moseley has used her and has been very happy with her temps. We're killing ourselves around here and it will be weeks before we get out from under it if we don't do something. How do I get in touch with Angie?" asks Sara, sounding excited.

"I'll e-mail you her number. In the meantime, I'll call Angie and fill her in on the situation so when you call she'll know some background. It'll save you a little time."

"Mark, thanks a million!"

"Glad to do it, Sara. Got anything else on your plate I can help with?"

"You've already been a huge help! Can I do anything for you?"

"I'm in good shape, Sara, but thanks for asking. If you need anything else, just give me a shout."

"Thanks for giving me some hope," Sara's voice sounds noticeably more relaxed. "Have a wonderful week."

Mark hangs up the phone. After a quick click in his ACT! database, he retrieves Angie's number and gets ready to call his friend with a referral.

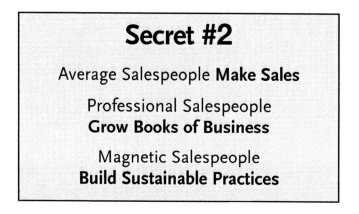

▶ Average Salespeople Make Sales

Alex is an Average salesperson. His focus is on the sale and getting it closed. He has a transaction mentality. Like other Average salespeople, he is interested in making a sale and moving on to the next one. Average salespeople typically spend their days bounding from one sales opportunity to the next.

They spend inadequate time developing relationships before or after the sale. When they do follow-up, their motives are often transparent, like Alex's was with Mr. Baldwin. Alex's intent was to secure referrals. He even came right out and asked for them!

Of course, Alex has been taught to do this by his sales manager and it is what everyone else in his company does. What Alex has not figured out is that nobody likes to be asked for referrals; even though most people are happy to volunteer them.

There is a big difference between asking for referrals and being given referrals voluntarily. When you ask for a referral, you are putting someone on the spot. It makes them uncomfortable and puts pressure on them to subject their friends and colleagues to a sales pitch.

Do you like receiving unsolicited calls from strangers, even if your buddy told them to call you? Few of us do. Why then do we think it is okay to ask for referrals, especially right after we have closed a sale? It comes across as pushy and presumptuous. That is not what Alex wants to be, but it is how he is perceived because of his actions. Like other Average salespeople, Alex is more concerned with himself and his sales numbers than with his client and their relationships. And the client knows it. Do you think Alex's client, Mr. Baldwin, will take his call so readily next time?

Here is another way to think about it. Alex gave his client something of value—a new phone system— and his client gave Alex something in return—money. They are "even" in the transaction, each having received an equitable exchange of value. When Alex asks for a referral, he has tipped the scales and asked for more than he has earned. He is asking someone to help him out, without regard for making sure the other person is gaining anything in return.

Some people do not mind helping someone else out without an expectation of reciprocation. But what tips the scale is the fact that the client usually has much more to lose than he does to gain. Essentially, Alex is asking his client to "risk" damaging his long-standing relationships for him. If Alex screws up or the referred person feels like his time is being wasted, it is the client who loses face—not Alex. Most people are not willing to put their reputation on the line so early in the sales relationship; and they should not be expected or pressured to do so.

In addition to putting undue pressure on clients and prospects, Average salespeople's preoccupation with closing the sale has other negative consequences. They view selling as a high volume transaction game. They think they have to talk to lots of prospects, because only a small percentage will actually buy anything. In other words, their closing ratios stink. Ironic, since they are always trying to close the sale.

Their eagerness to make the sale leads to taking on anyone that will say yes — even when the fit is not right. Typically, Average salespeople are happy to over promise to make the sale. They will often let someone else in their organization worry about delivery and customer service issues after the sale is made. There is no sense in jeopardizing a sale with delivery or service issues, the Average salesperson rationalizes.

Like other Average salespeople, Alex's scattered approach to prospecting also impacts his client relationships. He takes what he can get and often ends up with clients he really does not like all that much. Consequently, the only thing he has in common with his clients is that they bought something from him. It is hard to develop a deep relationship when you have nothing to talk about except a transaction. Hence, client retention and referrals suffer.

▶ Professional Salespeople Grow Books of Business

Professional salespeople like Paula do not think and act like Average salespeople. Professionals think like business owners, and they understand it is important to keep their clients happy.

Professionals know it is easier to keep a client than to go out and get a new one. They build a book of business, a collection of clients and past clients who buy from them repeatedly. In addition to repeat business, they receive some decent referrals from satisfied clients. Professional salespeople stay in touch with each client in the hopes of generating future sales.

Paula has placed each client on a regular callback list. Between phone calls, she also demonstrates she cares by remembering clients' special dates and adding a personal touch on handwritten notes and cards.

Despite the common practice in her industry, Paula has veered away from directly asking for referrals. When she used to do it, it made her feel awkward and uncomfortable. She sensed the same reaction from her clients. Since then, she discovered that if she takes care of her clients, most of them will take care of her.

When she schedules her annual reviews, the focus is on her products and services and making sure her clients are well taken care of on that front. Most of her annual reviews turn into sales opportunities as she spots areas for additional coverage. That is great for her and it helps her client, but it is not enough. With her focus on what she can personally do to help the clients, some of her clients perceive her visits as sales calls. When they are feeling tapped out by her, they reject her reviews, even to their own detriment.

Paula also has a few clients in her book of business that really drag her down—folks like Mr. Mountcastle who do not value her advice, and who dictate to her how things are going to be. Rather than refer them to someone else in the office who might be a better fit, Paula allows them to control her way of doing business and ruin her mood. She would be better off letting them go than letting them drag her down.

In truth, Paula brings some of this on herself by the way she positions herself with her clients. Remember her thank you note? What was the tone of that letter? Was it one of happiness to be working together on an equal basis or was it one of gratitude and subservience? Paula mentioned several times how thankful she was that they chose her to work with. But did she not provide something valuable in return?

When Paula positions herself as someone who relies on the good graces of others to make her living, she places herself below them. She becomes subservient rather than a peer. A few simple and subtle changes like "I'm glad we're working together," instead of "Thank you for your business," will go further to establish peer-to-peer relationships and elevate her interactions with her clients.

▶ Magnetic Salespeople Build Sustainable Practices

Magnetic salespeople recognize these pitfalls of client interactions. In other words, they bring a different mindset to the table than most salespeople. They are rarely viewed as salespeople; instead they are perceived as valued resources. And because their value is not based solely on what they are selling, Magnets create strong peer-to-peer relationships with prospects and clients.

The type of extra value Magnets bring to their relationships is significant. For example, Mark has developed strong relationships with a large number of product and service providers and refers them to his clients. He truly cares about the long-term success of his clients, both personally and professionally. Mark knows that if he takes care of his clients, he will be rewarded willingly with all the referrals he needs. He knows his clients refer people to him not only because they want to help the person they are referring but because they truly want to help Mark, too. They care about him because he cares about them.

Mark has also realized the value of firing clients who are not a perfect fit for his practice. He spent time a few years ago deciding what kind of attributes he seeks in clients and what value he brings to them.

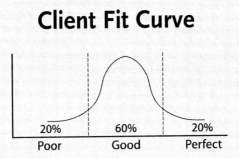

Client Fit Curve

20%	60%	20%
Poor	Good	Perfect

Most salespeople have clients that fit into three categories—poor-fit, good-fit and perfect-fit. Poor-fit clients are not satisfied with your product or service and will drain your time, resources and energy. Good-fit clients are content with your services and represent the majority of customers for most salespeople. Perfect-fit clients are loyal customers who provide ongoing business and referrals.

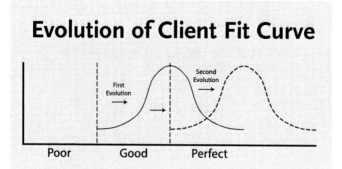

Evolution of Client Fit Curve

Poor   Good   Perfect

As you build your business, it is important to eliminate poor-fit clients. By doing this, you will have more time to build and cultivate relationships with good and perfect clients. Over time and as you continually refine your expertise and Bull's Eye Market, you will only have perfect-fit clients.

He sells only to those with the desired characteristics. Mark knows dealing with a difficult client is time he could better spend cultivating relationships with great clients. He would rather be on the golf course with a client and a great prospect than in the office dealing with someone who is not a good fit.

As their practices develop and mature, Magnetic salespeople become more and more selective. Not only do they eliminate poor-fit clients who zap their time and energy, they also critically evaluate their prospects before they become clients. The sales process becomes a mutual evaluation. Only those prospects that are the right fit become clients. In turn, Magnetic salespeople are able to maintain and grow their practices primarily through repeat business and referrals.

A Magnetic salesperson's prospecting and selling methodology is like good farming. A smart farmer will take time to choose the right plot of land. He will cultivate and nourish the soil and wisely choose the highest quality seeds. Once the seedlings sprout, he fertilizes and protects them from the elements. He also weeds out the weak plants, knowing they will rob the stronger ones of nutrients and prevent them from thriving. After a good harvest he will reinvest in the land. He knows the land will bear crops year after year if he takes care of it.

A Magnetic salesperson treats his business in the same manner, cultivating his territory and his clients. He is not afraid to "weed out" prospects or clients who turn out to be the wrong fit. He understands the opportunity cost of poor-fit clients. As a result, his clients come to trust him at ever deepening levels and he continues to do business in increasing amounts.

Magnetic salespeople are concerned with making sure their clients are the right fit on three different levels in a business-to-business selling environment: personal fit, company fit and wants fit. In business-to-consumer selling, personal fit and wants fit are critical.

Webster defines practice as "the continuous exercise of a profession." The concept is not a new one. Other professional service providers have been farming for years. They refer to it as "building practices" and are so good at it that many partners and owners are able to sell their practices when they are ready to retire.

Summary

To become more Magnetic, you should:

- Be a valued resource to your clients and prospects.

- Make sure you have the right clients.

- Establish peer-to-peer relationships with others.

- Engage in a mutual evaluation process between buyer and seller.

- Eliminate poor-fit clients.

CHAPTER 4

Connectivity or Bust

▶ Alex — The Average Salesperson

It is Wednesday morning. "Thank goodness I have some appointments today. At least I'm out doing what I do best, talking to prospects," Alex says to himself. He sings to the music blasting out of his radio. "I love this part of my job, out on the road; I've got my coffee and my music." He laughs, "This would be a great job if it weren't for the customers. Well, maybe it's not the customers. It's being stuck in the office making calls with Jerry breathing down my neck." Alex's thoughts turn to his prospect as he pulls into the parking lot of Beach Manufacturing. "I wonder what this Mr. Collie is like."

"Hi, I'm Alex from PhoneMax. It's nice to meet you Mr. Collie," says Alex, shaking hands and walking into the Controller's office.

"Come in, Alex, and have a seat. Glad to meet you too," he replies.

"Wow, that's a huge fish on the wall! Where did you catch it? I love to fish too! Are you into fishing?" asks Alex, seeking to build a little rapport before beginning his presentation.

"No, someone gave that to me and I thought it was interesting so I stuck it up there. My wife won't have it in the house," chuckles Mr. Collie. Mr. Collie studies Alex and knows he has another one. He has grown weary of telling his fishing tales to every salesperson that walks in the door. The fact is, he did catch the fish. But over time, he has learned he can save a lot of senseless chatter with a response like the one he gave Alex. Besides, he finds it fun to watch salespeople squirm a little.

"Well, it sure is impressive," replies Alex, somewhat taken aback. He was hoping to talk about fishing a bit and get on Mr. Collie's good side.

"So, Alex, what did you want to see me about today? You mentioned phone systems in your call and we're looking at them right now, so it was good timing."

"Well, we've got all sorts of phone systems from basic two-line models up to ones that will actually track your outbound calls so you can monitor your people's activity. But before I tell you about them, may I ask a few questions?" asks Alex.

"Sure, Alex, fire away," answers Mr. Collie, settling back into his chair.

Alex runs through the mental checklist of the different needs assessment questions in his arsenal. "First of all, what do you like about your current system and provider?"

"Our current folks have been good to us. They recommended a system about five years ago that has served us well, but we've doubled the company since then, and we've really outgrown our four-line system. It was expensive at the time, but it served its purpose well."

"What do you not like about your current system?" asks Alex, mentally checking off the questions in his head.

"As I said, we've outgrown it. It worked well, but now we have to put too many people on hold and I'm afraid we're losing some of them."

"Do you think that saving money on your new system would be good?" asks Alex, anticipating a hearty yes.

"Well of course. What kind of businessman would I be if I didn't want to save money?" responds Mr. Collie curtly.

"If I can show you a system that does everything you want and will save you some money, will you buy it?" Alex remembers the ABC's of selling as his boss Jerry frequently calls it—"always be closing."

"Well, we're going to look at all of our options. Why don't you just tell me about the things you offer?" Mr. Collie shifts back in his seat.

"Sure," says Alex. "We've got over 80 different models with all kinds of features. Let me tell you about our most popular one, the XL400. I've got some information here. Let me show you what it can do." Alex pulls out a notebook with brochures, spec sheets, pictures and feature lists. He very carefully explains the features and benefits to Mr. Collie, demonstrating his years of experience in the telecom industry.

After about 12 minutes, Mr. Collie interrupts, "Well, Alex it sounds like you really know your stuff. Can you get me a proposal on that system? It sounds like it will do everything we need. My assistant Eileen will get you any information you need from us. Thanks for coming in today," he says as he rises, "I'll look for that proposal."

Alex is elated as he leaves the building. That was really easy. The guy wanted a proposal right away! He starts adding up the number of phones, the amount of features he is going to suggest, and the price of each item. "This is going to be one big order," Alex screams over the music in the car as he rushes back to the office to start crunching the numbers. As he sits at the stoplight, he starts calculating the size of the order he is going to put in the proposal and how much his commission will be for the sale. "I have got to get on this right now," he thinks. If he turns the proposal around quickly, he knows he will have a better shot at clinching the deal.

Alex's euphoria lasts only a few days. He sends his proposal to Mr. Collie and after several follow-up calls, he receives a voice mail message letting him know that Mr. Collie went with another provider.

"Man, that stinks!" fumes Alex. "I spent a lot of time on that proposal and that was a terrific system. It did everything he wanted and I even discounted the price. What a jerk. I'll bet he got something that won't do half of what mine will do. Some people just don't get it."

▶ Paula — The Professional Salesperson

Paula looks at the clock in her car as she pulls into the parking lot for her two o'clock appointment and thinks, "I made great time getting here. It's only 1:45. This should be a good appointment; let me look through my notes and research on CMT Company before I go in. Stan always refers me to great people." She makes a note in her Palm Pilot to send him a thank you note before heading inside to meet Maggi Turner.

"Good afternoon, Ms. Turner. It's a pleasure to meet you. Stan speaks highly of you and the business you've built," says Paula, introducing herself to the owner of CMT Company.

"He says the same of you, Paula. Please call me Maggi. Let's sit down," answers the CEO.

"Thank you, Maggi. Tell me, how do you know Stan?"

"Stan and I go way back to college. We were both accounting majors at Tech until I realized I wasn't cut out for it and changed to business administration. He was always so good at the numbers that it made sense when I started my own business to hire him as my accountant. How do you know him?" asks Maggi.

"I met Stan at a networking event a couple of years ago. Over time, the more I got to know him, the more I liked him. And when I was looking for someone reputable to refer my clients to, well the rest is history," replies Paula. "What made you decide to start your own business?"

As Maggi tells a story of hard work and perseverance, Paula makes mental notes about Maggi's character and values. Paula continues asking questions about Maggi's business, including why she still works so hard and what she is trying to accomplish in the long run.

"What I'd really like to do is sell this place and

retire in about 10 years," Maggi shares. "I'm getting too old for the daily grind and I'd really like to travel more than I am able to now."

"Where would you go and what would you do?" asks Paula, wanting to understand Maggi's motivations.

Maggi tells Paula about her hopes and dreams and all the places she will go and things she will do when she retires. It seems she has put a lot of thought into her plans and is serious about pursuing them.

"It sounds like you know what you want, Maggi. Tell me, what have you done so far to make your plans a reality?"

Maggi shares her past attempts at planning and her current portfolio of investments and insurance. Paula takes out her needs analysis sheet and jots down all the relevant information, prompting Maggi about products as necessary.

"That's a pretty good start on planning. I commend you on the job you've done so far. Our firm has some ideas about how to put everything together. May I show you some of our philosophies?" Paula brings out a small binder with several charts, graphs and pie charts illustrating appropriate ways of accumulating and protecting assets. Maggi seems interested and follows the presentation.

After she is done, Paula asks, "So what questions do you have for me?"

"I'm not sure I have any questions. It seems like you really know your stuff and that you understand me and my business. Could you work up a proposal on the things you recommend, then come back and show me what you've got? I'm ready to get this underway and Stan says you're the one to use, so let's do it."

As Paula drives back to the office, she reviews her meeting with Maggi in her mind to make sure that everything went as expected. Paula feels confident about closing the business. Stan is a great referral source. Maggi is just the kind of client Paula is looking for.

▶ Mark—The Magnetic Salesperson

Mark is on his way into Brenda's office. Brenda Griffith is the Marketing and Client Services Manager at the law firm of Parker, Dorotich and Curran. She was referred to Mark by one of his clients, Gus Godfrey, and she is anxious to meet with him.

"Good afternoon Brenda. It's nice to meet you. Gus speaks highly of you." Mark shakes Brenda's hand.

"Glad to meet you Mark. Gus says you do great work and that you know more than anyone else in this town about printing. I sure could use the help." She pulls out a chair for him and they sit at the conference table.

Mark begins his conversation with Brenda in much the same way Paula did with Maggi. He asks questions about Brenda's professional background as well as her plans for the future. He learns what she has accomplished in her career in addition to how she wants to make her mark in the future.

With his inquisitive and natural conversational style, Brenda finds herself sharing things with Mark that she does not usually share. The conversation is easy and Brenda enjoys the sincere interest Mark is showing her.

Beyond testing for personal fit, Mark also finds out about the firm's history and its future plans.

"Mark, tell me about what you do and how you do it," Brenda injects.

"What would you like to know?" asks Mark in response.

"Well, how did you get to your position? You come so highly recommended, how did you get to that place?"

Mark tells a brief story about how he has focused on the legal marketing field for years and how he has enjoyed working with law firms. Brenda nods as she senses his expertise. She is used to dealing with printing reps who are jacks-of-all-trades.

"I'm convinced," says Brenda. "What can you do for us?"

"Brenda, I'm really not sure at this point. I don't know enough about what you need or how you like to work. Would you mind if we spend some more time evaluating each other to make sure what I do is what you need and vice versa? I'd hate to discover that in the middle of a project," replies Mark.

"No one has ever turned down a sure sale from me before. OK, let's talk. Ask whatever you like," answers Brenda, sitting back in her chair.

"Brenda, why do you really care what printer you use? Why does it matter to you?"

"I'll tell you. I've been in the business for 16 years and I've suffered the wrath of many a partner who didn't get his materials when he wanted or there was some other delivery problem. Every printer I've worked with has promised to make me look good and every one has failed somewhere along the line.

I'm tired of taking the heat for a printer's mistakes. I just want someone I can count on so I can spend my time on more important matters."

"Is there anything else?" asks Mark, intently listening to her reply.

"There is one more thing. Our firm is thinking of opening an office in Florida and relocating some of its staff. I want to be one of those people. I love Florida and have always wanted to live there but couldn't afford the move. The firm would pick up all the expenses and I'd get a raise to boot. The only way I can get there is to be better at my job. If I have to waste time doing a printer's job for him, I can't get to the important stuff." Brenda pauses and says, "Please keep that confidential. You're the only person outside of my family who knows that."

"Of course I will. What else should I know?" asks Mark.

Mark and Brenda spend another 25 minutes talking about the types of printing Brenda's firm does, their typical deadlines, etc. Before Mark leaves, he sets another appointment with Brenda to discuss the details of a big project she has coming up next month.

As Mark drives away, Brenda picks up the phone and calls Gus to thank him for referring such a refreshing young man.

Secret #3
Average Salespeople **Manipulate**
Professional Salespeople **Communicate**
Magnetic Salespeople **Connect**

▶ Average Salespeople Manipulate

Alex did not grow up wanting to be a salesman. He just sort of fell into it. Throughout his life, people have told him he'd be great in sales because he can talk to anyone. And talk he has. Alex is like other Average salespeople; he has a big problem when he interacts with prospects and clients—he "pukes" on them. As you can probably guess, it is not pleasant for the prospect and it kills Alex's sales results. No, he does not empty the contents of his stomach on people; he empties the contents of his mind on them.

Alex, like other Average salespeople, believes his job is to talk to people and tell them what they need to know in order to buy from him. He is always thinking of new and cleverer ways to convince people what is good for them (and him!). When a prospect asks a simple question and sometimes even before, Alex launches into a lengthy narrative, telling the prospect everything he knows about the subject. He talks and talks, scarcely pausing for breath in the hopes he will make the sale on volume of product knowledge. When he does pause, it is usually because

---

he is trying to think of the next thing to say. He knows he should listen better but finds it difficult to both listen to what is being said to him and think of a good response at the same time.

As if puking were not bad enough, Average salespeople have other communication challenges. They have been taught to ask questions, but they ask the wrong questions. Not only do they ask the wrong questions, they ask them in the wrong way.

Average salespeople combine puking and asking questions. In other words, they ask run-on questions or a series of questions without pausing to give the prospect a chance to respond to each individual question. An example would be, "Mr. Prospect, what would you say your biggest challenge is? You mentioned that you had a problem with turnover. Is that your biggest problem? And if it is, what have you done about it so far?"

In this example, the prospect is bombarded with three questions and a statement. Usually, this kind of run-on questioning demonstrates to the prospect that the salesperson is not all that interested in the answers. The salesperson is not stopping to wait for an answer before moving on to the next question.

Sometimes, when an answer is solicited and given, the salesperson moves directly to the next question without probing for clarification. Even worse, because the salesperson is questioning skills are deficient, the next question asked does not follow a logical progression. The salesperson's random questioning is both distracting and annoying.

Because they do not have strong questioning skills, Average salespeople can end up with awkward silence when meeting with prospects. Since they have the tendency to "puke," an Average salesperson will fill the void by "telling and selling" instead of asking the right questions.

If they are not "telling and selling," Average salespeople often use their time with prospects "showing." They pull out their brochures, catalogs, portfolios and products. They use these visual aids as props and crutches to mask their poor sales skills. Of course, they do not realize that their approach is flawed.

Average salespeople fail to recognize that they are blowing their best opportunity to connect with their prospects, because most of them will not get a second chance. Time spent telling or showing is time not spent finding out what is important to the prospect. Prospects do not care how wonderful and diverse your portfolio is. They care about what you can do for them. Average salespeople often miss the chance to find out by not asking the right questions.

If they do ask questions, Average salespeople have a tendency to ask ammunition questions. In other words, they ask questions that will help them gather information in order to uncover a prospect's hot buttons with the sole intent of using the newly acquired information to back their prospects into a buying corner. No matter how a prospect responds, he feels pressured by the questioning. Typically, this results in the buyer giving curt or guarded responses.

Information questions, on the other hand, are used to gain unbiased understanding. Information questions seek the truth, while ammunition questions seek the sale. Alex was taught to ask ammunition questions in order to restate them later and use the prospect's own answers to force a decision. His boss has said a hundred times, "Never ask a question unless you already know the answer." That is not selling, that is manipulation.

One of Alex's favorite lines is, "Do you think saving money is good?" Of course the answer has to be "yes" unless the prospect wants to look like a complete idiot. Who wants to waste money? Alex always knows what his next question will be too: "Well, if I could show you something that would do that for you, would you buy it?" These sound like words you would hear coming from a used car salesman.

Alex thinks he has them cornered with that last "used car salesperson" question. How can they say no? If they admit that saving is good, they would be stupid not to buy. Or at least, that is Alex's logic. Unfortunately for Alex, it does not usually turn out that way. Instead, he is likely to get a brush-off like "I have to think about it" or "Can you get me a proposal?" at the end of his appointment.

The reason for the brush-off is because if the prospect agrees with a "yes" to an ammunition question, he is agreeing to a purchase before he has enough information to make an educated decision. If he does not buy later, then he contradicts himself. The prospect is trapped in a no-win situation, forced there by manipulative questioning. It may result in a quick sale once in a while for the Average salesperson, but it will destroy any hope of building long-term relationships, repeat sales and referrals.

Ammunition Versus Information Questions

Ammunition Questions:

These are questions that back a prospect into a corner and are used later as ammunition against the prospect. In other words, the answers to these questions are used to manipulate the prospect to buy. For example, getting the prospect to answer a series of questions with "yes" is a typical ploy used. This type of questioning will not build strong relationships with prospects and should not be used, even though it is a common practice of Average salespeople.

Information Questions:

These are questions designed to get a better understanding of the prospect and his situation, without inducing sales pressure. This type of questioning allows the prospect to relax and share more freely because there is no pressure exerted. In addition, information questions are generally open-ended to encourage a more meaningful conversation with the prospect. Information questions are used by Magnetic salespeople.

Examples of Ammunition and Information Questions include:

Ammunition: "What do you like most about your current vendor?"

Information: "What is critical to your satisfaction with this service?"

Ammunition: "What do you like least about your current vendor?"

Information: "What are your areas of concern regarding this service?"

Ammunition: "Is saving money important to you?" After prospect answers in the affirmative, "If I can show you a way to save money, will you buy today?"

Information: "What's important to you regarding _____?" After prospect answers, probe "Why is that?"

Ammunition: "What features are you looking for?"

Information: "What do you want to accomplish?"

Ammunition: "Are you the decision-maker?" or "Who makes the decision on this type of purchase?"

Information: "How are decisions handled in your company/your department/your family?"

Not only do Average salespeople ask pressure-inducing ammunition questions, they rarely take the time to connect on a personal level with their prospects. When they walk into a prospect's office, they scan the room for the fish-on-the-wall, the picture of the family or the golf clubs in the corner. They think if they can find something to talk about with some friendly banter, they can gain instant "rapport."

What they fail to realize is that every other salesperson who has walked in the decision-maker's office has done the same thing. Welcome to Vendorville.

What is Vendorville?

Vendorville is a place where 75%–80% of all sales-people live. Most salespeople feel stuck here and do not know how to leave.

Buyers and sellers are NOT on equal footing in Vendorville. In fact, if you are a salesperson in Vendorville, you will always be subservient to the buyers. Buyers will treat you like any other vendor and they will be more concerned with your price and terms than the unique value you provide. Salespeople stuck in Vendorville do not even realize that their actions keep them there and that there are other places they could live.

Vendorville is a place populated by Average salespeople. It is a place where the buyer says, "Jump!" and the salesperson says, "How high?" More commonly, however, the buyer says, "Lower your price if you want my business." and the salesperson says, "How low do I need to go?" You do not want to live in Vendorville. Average salespeople get stuck there with their transaction mentality, commodity mindset and inability to connect and build value-based relationships.

Alex lost the sale with Mr. Collie when he was asked for a proposal. Whether Mr. Collie did it to get Alex to stop talking or whether Alex offended him with the ammunition questions is a toss up. The end result is the same. It is another lost sales opportunity for Alex after hours of work. Buyers like Mr. Collie have dealt with lots of Average salespeople. They know that requesting a proposal is an effective ploy to get a salesperson out of their office.

Like Alex, Average salespeople are excited by being asked for a proposal. It certainly is a buying signal. Average salespeople fail to ask specific questions about what their prospects want in the proposal. So they end up with a proposal that is not aligned with the expectations of the prospect. For example, most salespeople have not discussed pricing or budgets until they deliver the proposal. If they are off the mark, they have wasted lots of time on a proposal and reduced the probability of getting the business. This can be avoided with better and more in-depth questioning on the front end.

Average salespeople are poor listeners, although they rarely recognize this deficiency in themselves. They do not realize that they cannot listen and talk at the same time. If they spend most of their time showing and telling, their listening surely suffers. What they should do is apply the 80/20 rule during their initial prospect meetings. The salesperson should be asking questions and listening 80% of the time, and talking 20% of the time.

Usually, Average salespeople zero in on their "needs assessment." They listen for the prospect to mention a "hot button" issue and then leap into action, telling the prospect how their product or service is "the solution." Despite what Average salespeople believe, this is not a good way to sell.

▶ Professional Salespeople Communicate

Professional salespeople approach their interactions with prospects differently than Average salespeople.

Professionals understand that people hate to be sold but love to buy. As a result, they spend their time communicating with their prospects on a deeper and more personal level. They find out what is important to their prospects before offering solutions.

A Professional salesperson will ask numerous questions, probing deeper and deeper into the prospect's mind, and she will not stop until she is convinced she thoroughly understands just what the prospect wants. She asks questions to gather the information she needs to make sure the prospect can make an informed decision about buying. By doing so, she ensures there will be no buyer's remorse later on. In addition, she is positioning herself for future referrals because of her professional demeanor. Her prospects never feel overt sales pressure from her questioning.

One of Paula's favorite questions is "Do you consider saving money for retirement important?" Her next question, regardless of the answer is "Why?" While she might believe that saving is important, she never assumes it is important to the prospect. She has one client who did not believe saving for retirement was important because no one in his family lived past 60 years old. He did not think he was going to live that long either. Paula asked him more and more questions, and after a lengthy discussion, the prospect realized that his retirement was not important to him, but that his family's security was. He started a savings plan and added to his insurance coverage.

Like other Professionals, Paula knows how to dig deeper after her prospect answers her original questions. She probes below the surface for a full understanding of the situation. Paula understands that people rarely divulge their biggest hopes, fears and desires right away and that to truly help her prospects, she must understand them. Her approach yields sales results far better than those of the Average salesperson.

▶ Magnetic Salespeople Connect

Magnetic salespeople take their communication to the deepest level. They work to enhance their connection with customers. They go beyond asking great questions to test for fit and understand needs. They also get to the "emotional" wants of their prospects.

Magnets are able to get their prospects to open up through a combination of good questioning and skilled listening. Good questioning always starts with building the relationship through appropriate personal fit questions.

By understanding the prospect and what's important to her, the Magnetic salesperson establishes a "real" rapport at a meaningful and authentic level. More importantly, by connecting at this level in the beginning of the relationship, the Magnet is able to get the prospect to open up and share at a much greater depth. This is critical when the salesperson gets to the point in the conversation when determining needs and wants is important. An Average salesperson may come to understand basic "factual" needs; a Magnetic salesperson is able to dig to the "emotional" wants of the prospects. The Magnet knows that people buy based on their emotions and he is skillful in uncovering what is important to his prospects and why.

Prospects are willing to share more of their emotional wants with a Magnet because they feel a connection. Prospects connect when the salesperson demonstrates through his words and actions that he sincerely cares about them and not just what they can do for him. Prospects want to work with someone who understands them and is concerned in helping them. Starting with personal fit questions is a great way to begin the process.

Personal Fit Questions

In order to develop a meaningful relationship, start by asking questions that help you understand the other person. While these questions are personal in nature, they are not so personal that they are uncomfortable for the prospect. The prospect's responses will naturally lead you to additional questions.

Examples of good Personal Fit Questions include:

- How did you get in your current position?
- How long have you been with the company/in your position?
- What did you do prior to joining this organization?
- Where do you want to go from here?
- What's going to help get you there?
- Is there anything that's getting in your way?
- What keeps you motivated?

Magnets also divulge information that will help their prospects make the best decision, whether with them or their competitors. They would rather turn away business than take business that is not the best fit for them or their prospects. They have stopped trying to be all things to all people.

For example, Mark freely refers business to other companies that will complement his print offerings. Often, what a prospect or client thinks he wants is not best for him; Mark's candid and honest feedback makes him a valuable resource and advisor.

Mark generally starts his questioning with something like, "Mr. Prospect, how did you get to your current position?" He continues asking questions designed to inform him about the person behind the desk. Mark knows that if he is going to build a long-term relationship with someone, he wants it to be with someone that he likes and respects. Mark does not need a list of pre-determined questions. He has gotten to the point in his career where the questions flow naturally. All he really has to do is remain interested and the next question comes effortlessly. He finds himself having fun and stimulating conversations every time he meets with someone new.

Magnets know that if they take care of people, the money will take care of itself. So there is never a sense of sales pressure, overt or subtle. As a result, they never worry about where they are "in the sales process." Magnetic salespeople simply continue to engage their prospects until they have asked all the questions they need to fully evaluate the situation. At that point, most of their appointments result in a final question from the prospect: "How do we work together?"

The questioning skills of Magnetic salespeople are so effective, in part, because of their exceptional listening skills. They maintain strong eye contact, use appropriate body language and really hear what their prospects say. They use clarifying and probing questions to dig deeper for a fuller understanding and connection. Unlike Average salespeople that tend to talk too much in an initial meeting with a prospect, Magnetic salespeople follow the W.A.I.T. approach.

W.A.I.T.—Why Am I Talking?

When you are meeting with a prospect, you should be asking information questions and listening. Avoid the temptation to tell the prospect about all the products or services you can offer. Your prospect does not care about everything you can do. He cares about how you can help him. You will not know how you can help unless you are getting the right information from your prospect. So, fight the urge to talk, remember to W.A.I.T.

There are two times when you should talk in an initial meeting with a prospect:

• When you are asking a question

• When you are answering a direct question

Otherwise, sit back and LISTEN!

In the earlier scenario, Mark actually enhanced his connection with Brenda when he rebuffed her attempt to turn him into another print vendor and reasserted his belief in making sure the fit was right for both them. As a result, she shared some very important insights with him which will allow him to give her exactly the type of service she needs to reach her goals. In exchange, Mark will reach his goals.

Summary

To become more Magnetic, you should:

- **Start building the relationship by understanding the person and testing for personal fit.**

- **Ask information questions, not ammunition questions.**

- **Seek a thorough understanding of your prospects that goes below their surface needs to their emotional wants.**

- **Listen intently and let the conversation develop naturally.**

- **Focus your attention on the prospect, not your product.**

- **Demonstrate competence by asking the right questions, not telling and showing.**

- **Recognize that prospects care less about what you do and how you do it than how you can help them. Speak to their benefits, not your features or processes.**

C H A P T E R • 5

Who Loves You Baby?

▶ ## Alex — The Average Salesperson

The local Chamber of Commerce is having an "after-hours" mixer on Thursday evening. Alex knows that networking is a great way to meet prospects, so he is headed to the event. He has not been to a Chamber function in several months, and he hopes this event is more productive than the last one he attended.

Alex arrives at the Chamber mixer right on time. He is surprised to see a line of attendees snaking out the door. He thinks to himself, "Well, at least I should be able to find some people to talk to. I wonder who I can sell something to?" He gets in line to check in at the registration table. As he writes his name on a name tag, he decides not to add his company name. Who knows, if he is lucky he might overhear some competitors talking.

Alex gets a drink and meets Jay in the line at the bar. "I sell phone systems," replies Alex, when Jay asks what he does.

"Oh, do you know John Broderson at Alpha Systems?" asks Jay, mentioning the person from whom he bought his phone system a few years ago.

"No, I don't. We don't run across Alpha much. Their systems don't really compare to ours," Alex replies.

There is an awkward pause. "Um, well then, what sort of companies do you work with? I mean, who are your customers?" asks Jay, not knowing where else to go with the conversation.

"My customers are typically companies who are moving or growing fast and need to expand," replies Alex, hoping Jay might be in the market himself or know of someone who is. Alex digs into his pocket for a business card to present to Jay but remembers he ran out earlier in the day and forgot to restock before he left the office.

"That's interesting," says Jay, as he starts glancing around the room.

"Yeah, we've got customers all over the map. Anyone who needs a new phone system is a great prospect for us."

Jay asks, "Is there a certain size company that is the best for your phone systems?"

"Big, small, it doesn't matter, we can help anyone. We've got great prices so everybody can afford us and we have great service, too" Alex responds, not recognizing that Jay has already lost interest in their conversation.

"Why does this always happen?" thinks Alex after he has gotten his drink and Jay has excused himself. Alex recognizes a buddy across the room and heads over to see Dave. At least they can talk about last night's game.

▶ Paula — The Professional Salesperson

Paula has invited Stan, one of her referral sources from The Four Amigos to the Chamber mixer. As they enter the room, Stan spots someone he knows and asks Paula if she knows him. When she says she does not, Stan takes her over to introduce her.

"Hi, Jay, how's it going?" asks Stan, shaking Jay's hand.

"Fine, fine, business is up so things look great. How about you?" replies Jay, glancing at Paula.

"Things are going well with me, too. I love it when tax season is over! Jay, do you know Paula Henson?" Stan introduces them.

"What do you do Paula?" asks Jay.

"I work with small business owners to make sure they can pass on their business to whom they want, when they want," Paula says easily.

"That sounds interesting. How do you do that?"

"Paula, let me answer that," Stan interrupts. "This woman is a whiz with financial plans. She and I work very closely together with some of my clients and they think she is amazing."

"So, why have you been keeping her from me Stan? Don't I rank?" Jay laughs as he gives Stan a friendly nudge. "Paula, perhaps you and I should talk later. I own a small plumbing company, and I'd really like to hand it over to my son someday," Jay replies.

"I would enjoy finding out more about your business, Jay."

He reaches into his pocket and hands Paula his card. "Why don't you give me a call and we can set up a time to talk. Do you have a card?"

Paula hands her card to Jay and promises to call to make an appointment.

▶ Mark—The Magnetic Salesperson

Mark is attending the monthly Legal Marketing Association meeting. He has brought two guests—Erika and Dan—with him, both new Marketing Coordinators for firms he works with.

"Erika and Dan, I'm glad you could make it tonight. The LMA has a great group of people and I think you'll enjoy meeting them. Is there anyone in particular you know you want to meet?" asks Mark as they stand in line at the registration table.

"None that I can think of Mark. I'm too new to know who's who yet," Dan answers. Erika nods in agreement.

"That's fine. I'd like you to meet the president, Peter Roman, and a few members of the board. I'd also like to find Steve Verdillo, head of membership. He knows everyone and can tell you all about the association. It's really a worthwhile group to join."

At the check-in table, Mark recognizes Mary, the secretary of the group, overseeing registration.

"Hi, Mary. How are you doing? I'd like you to meet my guests this evening, Erika Brandt and Dan Kellerman. Erika and Dan, this is Mary Walls, our chapter's illustrious and hard-working Madame Secretary." Mary smiles back at Mark.

He continues, "Mary, Erika is Cindy's new replacement over at Whitlow and Besosa and Dan just transferred from the Raleigh office of Moore, Hilyer & Ishman." Mark looks at his two guests and says, "Mary is incredible, she keeps our group organized."

The newcomers smile and exchange greetings with Mary.

"Mary, is Peter here yet? I want to introduce him to Erika and Dan," Mark asks.

"He's up near the stage. Go on over, I'll get you signed in. Erika and Dan, Mark has taken care of your registration and your name tags are right here. Enjoy the meeting and let me know if I can do anything for you."

Mark introduces Erika and Dan to the president and tells Peter how impressed he is with both of them. The group chats a bit more, exchanges cards and Mark takes the pair over to meet several more people. Throughout the evening, Mark accompanies them, and stands to introduce them as his guests during the official meeting.

After the event, both Dan and Erika are thrilled with the contacts they made. "Everyone was so friendly and helpful," remarked Erika as she and Dan say goodbye in the parking lot.

"Everyone sure likes Mark. He's a minor celebrity. We wouldn't have made nearly so many great contacts without his help," Dan responds.

"You're right about that," replies Erika.

On his drive home, Mark makes a mental note to follow-up with Erika and Dan in the morning with a quick call. Mark makes building relationships appear effortless and fun.

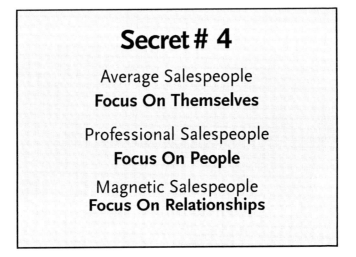

Secret # 4

Average Salespeople
Focus On Themselves

Professional Salespeople
Focus On People

Magnetic Salespeople
Focus On Relationships

▶ Average Salespeople Focus On Sales

Like many Average salespeople, Alex believes his job is to make sales. He comes to work each day wondering who he is going to close and how much money he will make doing it. He has even developed the habit of calculating his commission before he has even finished the appointment. In other words, it is all about him.

Unfortunately for Alex, selling never seems to get easier. When he started in his current position, he was told that within five years he would have enough customers so that he would have a steady stream of sales from repeat clients and referrals. That has not panned out, so Alex has supplemented his cold calling with some periodic networking events.

Networking has not worked well for Alex either. He checks the Chamber networking calendar periodically, but has not managed to be a regular attendee at any of the events. He has also attended some local networking meetings and tip groups. He has been to lots of meetings but not much has materialized.

What Alex has not realized is that everything is not about selling. Average salespeople are always in selling mode, hoping someone will jump up and buy from them. Their focus on the sales transaction makes them oblivious to the subtleties of building and nurturing relationships. In turn, they often sell like their product or service is a commodity. They sell on price and features, not value and benefits. In their minds, that is the quickest and easiest way to make the sale and help themselves.

The feedback that Average salespeople frequently give to their sales managers is "I can't sell more because our prices are too high." Yet, other salespeople in the office are hitting their quotas with better margins. It is usually not the pricing, but the salesperson's approach that needs overhauling.

That overhaul, in part, needs to be from an internal "me" focus to an external "you" focus. Average salespeople are always looking for what someone can do for them, instead of seeing what they can do for others. That is why they are always asking for referrals and feeling disappointed when they do not get them. They do not realize that the way to get them is not to ask, but to give to others first without expectations or pressure.

At the Chamber event, Alex could have easily asked Jay how he knew John Broderson. Instead, by undermining the competition, Alex turned Jay off and failed to engage in any meaningful conversation. That is because Alex was less concerned with connecting with Jay and more concerned with pushing his phone systems.

Beyond Alex's mishandling of the John Broderson reference, it would have been very appropriate for him to ask Jay what he did, how he got in his business, if he was a member of the Chamber, etc. Instead, Alex "puked" on Jay and lost an opportunity to connect with the owner of a growing business who is on the Chamber's board of directors.

▶ Professional Salespeople Focus on People

Paula and Stan strengthened their relationship by going to the networking event together and helped each other with some meaningful introductions. They were able to brag about each other and create some genuine interest.

Unlike Alex, Paula restrained from jumping on Jay when she discovered he was a great prospect for her. With Stan's help, she is ready to make an appointment that has some real potential.

As a Professional, Paula focuses on people and is mindful of engaging in conversations regardless of where they lead. If the opportunity presents itself, she wants to be ready. But her focus is on the other person and not herself. Her low-pressure approach is disarming to the people she meets.

By focusing on people, Professionals are able to engage in meaningful conversations that often lead to further opportunities. That is because people like to do business with other people that they like and respect. Even if opportunities do not manifest themselves immediately or at all, Professionals realize that the way they interact with others will impact their reputation.

▶ Magnetic Salespeople Focus On Relationships

Magnets, like Mark, take their relationship-building to an even higher level. They understand that every relationship is valuable, even ones with people who are not necessarily buyers. They spend time helping each person so they can become better and more connected to others.

At the LMA meeting, Mark spent his evening increasing his credibility not only with Erika and Dan, who will never forget his kindness as they grow in their careers, but also with Mary and Peter and other important members of the association. Mark is one of a few non-legal associate members who are welcomed with open arms at LMA events. Many of the others are treated like sharks and avoided.

Mark is welcomed because he is focused on helping others; a philosophy and practice that he shares with other Magnetic salespeople. It is the same philosophy of the largest networking organization in the world, Business Networking International (BNI). Their philosophy is "Givers Gain." It is an unspoken mantra of Magnetic salespeople as well. They know that by helping others, they will also succeed.

Sometimes there is not a direct cause and effect relationship—you help me, so I help you. It might be that you help Diana and Diana helps me and I help you. Magnets recognize that in the long run, what goes around comes around. Their good works will be rewarded, so it pays to give to others without any expectations of reciprocity.

Further, Magnetic salespeople protect the relationships they develop. They do this by open and honest communication, acting with integrity and standing behind their words. They know that anything less is disingenuous and harmful to building strong relationships. It is no surprise that Magnetic salespeople have unshakable loyalty and support from their clients, prospects and other relationships. People like to be around Magnets; Magnets attract others because they are externally focused. They give to others selflessly and generously. It is who they are.

Giving selflessly to others can be a challenging milestone for many salespeople to reach. Most of us have a built-in barometer that is constantly assessing, "What's in it for me?" That inward focus limits us, however. It insulates us. Instead, an outward focus connects us to others and allows us to have more meaningful relationships. And it is the value and strength of our relationships that separate Average, Professional and Magnetic salespeople.

Summary

To become more Magnetic, you should:

- **Act with integrity and honesty in all interactions with others.**

- **Protect and value relationships with others; do not do anything to harm your relationships.**

- **Help others without concern for what they can or will do for you in return.**

- **Look out for the best interests of others.**

- **Keep an external focus; be a servant leader.**

(C H A P T E R • 6)

No More Excuses

▶ Alex—The Average Salesperson

It is Friday, and Jerry Saunders, Alex's boss, is preparing for Alex's quarterly performance review. This is frustrating for Jerry. He likes Alex and wants him to succeed but it seems like each review is the same, year after year. Alex has a great work ethic and he is smart, but he does not improve much each year. He has lots of potential but he does not live up to it.

At 3:00 p.m., Alex steps into Jerry's office for his quarterly review. After exchanging a few pleasantries, Jerry says, "Well Alex, here we are again. How do you think the year is going so far?"

"It's going pretty well so far. I'm almost at quota and I've got some good things in the pipeline. I should hit last year's production, and with a little bit of luck, I could even do better," shrugs Alex.

"Why do you think your production is about the same as last year? You know you should be at 110%."

Jerry has put on his "boss voice" as Alex calls it. Sometimes, Jerry laughs and cuts up with the sales reps and the next minute, he is using his "boss voice" to act authoritative. Alex hates the "nice boss/mean boss" routine. It would be much easier if he chose to act in one way or the other. "Oh well, it looks like 'mean boss' is in the room," he thinks.

"Well, the economy is still struggling. Lots of people are telling me they're waiting to move their offices until their businesses pick up." Alex replies. "Besides, I'm just one guy. Sometimes there just isn't enough time in the day to do all the prospecting, paperwork and appointments on my plate. Some more marketing and advertising would really help make the phone ring. And I could cover a lot more ground if I wasn't stuck in the office on the phone all the time." Alex knows he sounds like he is making excuses, but darn it, it is the way he feels.

"Barring any new marketing on our part, what else do you think you can do to get above last year's quota by 10%?" Jerry asserts.

"I guess I could try making a few more calls. If I increase my calls by 10%, it stands to reason I could make more sales. I'll try to come in 30 minutes earlier and see if I can work them in."

"Alex, I know you're a hard worker; I've never doubted that. I'm just not sure why you don't sell more. You're here early most days and late just as often. Do you think some sales training would help? I can send you to some classes. What do you think?" says Jerry.

"I appreciate the offer, but I know how to sell. It's just this soft economy and the fact that not as many companies want to move or open new offices.

Plus, the phones we sold a couple of years ago were too good. Those things never seem to need to be replaced. I just need to work a little harder. I'll try to do better. If I just get better organized and stay focused, I'll pull it out," Alex replies.

"I have faith in you, Alex. Let's see where you are at the end of the month and we'll make some decisions then." Jerry stands to shake hands with Alex.

Alex leaves the office with a knot in his stomach. Jerry means well, but he has a way of making Alex feel like a loser. "What's wrong with making quota? What does he expect from me anyway? Every year, the bar gets raised. I'm good at my job, I work hard, my clients like me. I can't help it that people aren't buying," Alex thinks. He grabs his coat and heads for the front door. He mutters to Katie at the front desk that he is gone for the afternoon on an appointment.

▶ Paula — The Professional Salesperson

Paula's manager, Ron, is preparing for his quarterly review with Paula. "This one is always easy," thinks Ron. "Paula is on track to hit her goals, she's number two in the office and she's great to work with. She's really supportive of me and backs me up on tough decisions. This won't take long at all."

"So, Paula, how do you think you're doing so far this year?" asks Ron.

"So far, pretty good. I'm on pace to hit my goal this year, which is 15% higher than last year's production. And I finished my CFP designation, which I know I can leverage into some good marketing exposure. I'm going to hit my goal this year for sure," she answers.

"You haven't let me down yet," smiles Ron.

"You know, Ron, I was thinking. Now that I'm not studying for my exam any longer, I'm going to have more time to really prospect. I'm going to increase my goal another 5% for next quarter. I really want new furniture for the living room and that will help me do it."

"I'll add your additional production to my planning." Ron replies. "So, how do you think you've progressed since our last review?" Ron asks, remembering he has to ask all his questions, even of Paula.

"I checked my notes from our last meeting and I accomplished all the things you asked me to. I took your suggestion about taking a class in etiquette and one in presentation skills and they're really paying off. I'm more confident in my skills. I also took to heart your idea of hiring an assistant and I've started the search for one as you know. It will really free me up to do more prospecting and less paperwork. Thanks for the suggestions," replies Paula, feeling glad she's got a manager who supports her with good ideas.

"Well, Paula, I guess there's not much else to say except keep up the good work. Let me know if there's anything I can do to help you reach your target this year," Ron says, shaking Paula's hand and smiling.

As Paula leaves she thinks to herself, "This really is a great place to work and I have some great customers that keep helping me grow my business. Now, I wonder what color sofa I should get?"

▶ Mark—The Magnetic Salesperson

Linda Bragg, the owner of Frank & Williams Printing, is preparing for her performance review with Mark. They are meeting at Chef Blair's, a local restaurant that is one of Mark's favorites. "Reviews with Mark are always fun," thinks Linda. "It's good to get out of the shop once in awhile and Mark always has some interesting ideas on how to market himself and the company. Oh good, a front space," Linda thinks as she pulls into the parking lot. Mark should arrive shortly; he is coming directly from an appointment with Donnie Malloy at Cowan and Sylvester.

Over appetizers Linda inquires, "Mark, what's on your plate for the next quarter?"

"I'm excited about the next few months, Linda" replies Mark. "I'm adding a new column to my e-newsletter. As you know, I write all the articles right now and they are all about marketing legal firms. Since I write them, they tend to have a slant towards print. And I'm adding a column that my friends Cristina and Jennifer are writing about web-marketing. It'll be a good addition to the print articles and I'm sure all of us will get more business from it."

Mark adds, "I've also made some great new contacts. My presentation at LMA last month really paid off. I already have seven new clients and I have another half-dozen that look promising just from that talk. I've even been approached to speak at the national meeting next June."

"As always, things sound great. What do you need from me to help out?" Linda asks of her top producer.

"I was thinking of doing a custom piece on our new digital press to show the LMA folks how it works. I'd like to do a personalized postcard for each person who attends next month's event. Mary will get me the attendee list and then I can get the cards printed. What do you think?" Mark asks.

"Great idea. Get with Kyra and work something up and we'll get it on the schedule. What else do you need?"

"The only other thing I can think of is I'd like a little special recognition for Sylvia. She works really hard for me and is a great assistant. You know I give her bonuses but I think it would mean a lot to her to be recognized by the company. Could you come up with something?" asks Mark.

"Sure. I can make that happen. We'll give Sylvia some recognition at the all-employee meeting next week. In fact, Lisette at Incentives Plus can help us with something special as a nice reward and thank you for a job well-done. I'm sure Sylvia will be thrilled. And I agree that it's well-deserved."

"That's perfect, Linda. Thanks," Mark responds.

"No, thank you Mark. Okay, enough about business, how are Maria and the kids?"

Mark and Linda spend a pleasant lunch talking about their families and their plans for upcoming vacations.

SECRET # 5

Average Salespeople **Try**

Professional Salespeople **Commit**

Magnetic Salespeople **Do**

▶ Average Salespeople Try

To understand the psyche of an Average salesperson, pay close attention to their language. They say things like "I'll try" or "I hope to." They have good intentions, or so it appears. The problem with their language is that it is wishy-washy.

By saying "try" and "hope" and "if," they give themselves a back-door escape route. In other words, they give themselves an out if things do not go as planned. It is the equivalent of standing with one foot on the dock and one foot in the boat. You can stand there balancing yourself, but there is a strong likelihood that you will end up all wet before it is over.

Average salespeople mean well, but their words show they have not truly committed. They perceive that the locus of control in their lives is with external forces and conditions. In other words, they will do their best but they cannot control what happens to them.

When they do not hit their sales goals, they always have lots of explanations and rationalizations. Stated differently, they have lots of excuses. You heard it from Alex when he met with his boss Jerry.

He blamed the struggling economy, not enough time, too much paperwork, not enough advertising and too much time stuck on the phone. And he perceived all those things to be beyond his control. By unconsciously putting all the responsibility for his success outside himself, he has made external circumstances predictors of his success.

By creating excuses and blaming, Alex has failed to take responsibility for his actions and his goals. He has become a victim. Of course, he tells Jerry that he'll "try" to do better. What do you think the likelihood is that he will actually change? It is not that he does not want to change. He simply does not know how to and does not believe he is the one in control. Until he changes his attitude and his beliefs, his behavior and his results will remain the same.

Alex, like other Average salespeople, also has not clearly established his priorities and he does not have an executable plan for achieving them. The excuses that he has identified are actually obstacles. Instead of addressing the obstacles and developing solutions, he has thrown up his arms and said, "I can't because…" Consequently, he has become reactive to his environment and is pulled in many directions. It is a stressful existence when you are stuck being the victim.

▶ Professional Salespeople Commit

Professional salespeople do not try; they commit. Making a commitment is the mental acknowledgement that this is something important. When Professionals make a commitment, whether to a client or to themselves, they see it through to the end. They have taken responsibility for the things that happen to them. They control their own destiny internally, rather than relying on external factors to help things go their way.

This is why Professionals seem to accomplish so much more than Average salespeople. They follow through on their ideas. They identify the things they want, set a plan to achieve them and execute the plan. No excuses, no whining. They hold themselves accountable for reaching the goals they want in life or find others to help them be accountable.

Professionals set their prospecting plan each day, decide whom to call and complete their plan. They even plan time into each day to handle unexpected difficulties. When their energy is flagging or they just cannot seem to get focused, they develop strategies to push forward.

Professionals speak a different language than Average salespeople. Instead of "I hope" or "I'd like to" or "I'll try," Professionals say, "I will," and "I can" and "when I do." There is little room for ambiguity in their language; they speak with conviction because they know they will accomplish most of the things they set their minds to. It takes willpower and concentration, but Professionals stick it out and as a result, accomplish their goals.

When Paula met with her boss, Ron, she did not make excuses. She did not have to. She had remained true to her goals and had accomplished the things that she wanted to accomplish. She was even planning to increase her goals because she wanted new living room furniture. She was willing to do what she needed to do to raise her revenue an additional 5%, because the reward for reaching her goal was important to her.

▶ Magnetic Salespeople Do

Magnets not only commit mentally, they are disciplined. That means that they do what they decide they need to do. And they do not let obstacles get in their way. In fact, they take 100% responsibility for everything in their lives. Even the obstacles.

That means that they identify the obstacles that can get in their way. Once identified, Magnets will come up with possible solutions to their obstacles. Once solutions are explored, the best ones will be selected and implemented. It is not that Magnetic salespeople have fewer obstacles than Average or Professional salespeople, they are just more determined and disciplined in addressing them. When they are challenged with an obstacle, they find a way to go up, over, around or through it.

For instance, you do not hear Mark making excuses. Instead, he is proactive. He sets goals and creates systems that will help him achieve his goals. He breaks his goals down into specific action steps and he blocks his time to make sure he stays on target.

In addition to setting goals and identifying obstacles, Mark examines the rewards and consequences of his goals to make sure he is focused on the right things. One of his rewards for staying focused and disciplined at work is to have more time with his family. He savors the time with his wife and children and makes them a priority in his daily plans. Mark has created goals for all areas of his life, not just his work. Achieving balance is critical to his overall contentment and happiness. He knows if his personal life is out of whack, it impacts his work performance and vice versa.

It appears that Mark's day is much less stressful and chaotic than that of many other salespeople. And it is. He has learned how to work smarter, not harder. It is not difficult either, since he has created the right habits.

Magnetic salespeople have moved beyond a conscious thought of being successful and accomplishing goals to an unconscious way of doing and being. They are dedicated to continuous improvement and growth. Magnetic salespeople seem to accomplish things effortlessly simply because it is their habit. It is their unconscious way of being that guides their behavior. All of their habits move them toward their goals and desires, never away from them. They practice the right things over and over until they are part of their routine, a part of who they are.

Their habits are fueled by their attitudes. Their thoughts are not limiting. In fact, their thoughts fuel their behavior and action. They are living the life they desire by design.

Mark is not only the top print salesman in his company, he is known and respected statewide within his Bull's Eye Market. It is no wonder that his boss and company owner, Linda, is eager to make sure his needs are being met. Star performers like Mark are a rare breed. He is a true Magnet.

Mark starts each day the same way, with a run through the neighborhood or a trip to the gym. He knows the regulars there and even has a few clients among them. He is well-known and respected for his disciplined approach to his health.

After a shower, shave and breakfast back at the house, Mark heads to the office at 8:00 a.m. He always has a smile on his face when he walks in because he knows it is going to be a great day. It always is. He is confident that there is nothing that can happen he cannot handle, and because he plans well, he knows what his day's activity looks like. He checks his calendar to make sure there is not too much to accomplish in one day and starts his activity.

Typically, he begins his work day with a few calls to clients to check in on them. If a referral presents itself, he immediately schedules a call on his calendar. He checks on his print jobs in production, then heads out for a networking event or prospecting meeting at lunch time. Afternoons often involve following through on referrals, preparing for speaking engagements, writing an article or strategizing with referral sources.

His days end when everything on his to-do list is completed, usually around 4:30 or 5:00 p.m. He heads home for dinner with the family, a ballgame with his kids or an evening out with his wife. Occasionally the family will join a client's family for dinner or a community event. Mark's business and personal lives are fully integrated with each other and they flow easily back and forth. His family is part of his career and they enjoy getting to know his clients and their families. Mark's life is exactly the way he chooses it to be.

Summary

To become more Magnetic, you should:

- Take 100% responsibility for everything in your life—the good and the bad.

- Identify obstacles, examine possible solutions and take action.

- Remain steadfast on achieving your goals despite distractions.

- Seek to understand your internal motivations.

- Reward yourself for your accomplishments.

- Create habits that perpetuate your personal and professional achievement.

- Maintain a positive attitude and strong belief in self.

- Prioritize those things that will move you closer to your goals.

- Eliminate or delegate activities that do not provide value.

CHAPTER • 7

Be a Lifer

▶ Alex—The Average Salesperson

Alex and Judy are headed to the beach for a week's vacation next week. Each year they go with another family, the DiAntonios.

"I've got the list of things to do for vacation, Alex," says Judy.

"Okay, give it to me. What's on it?" asks Alex, mentally gearing up for his chores. He looks forward to vacation, but sometimes all the work to get ready can be daunting. Alex gets lost in his thoughts, "It always seems like I spend the first three or four days trying to relax, and then before you know it, the week is over."

Alex becomes aware that Judy is talking to him. "Well, I've got a list of items to pack here. And we have to run to the warehouse store to get sodas, beer, lunchmeat, bread and chicken. And I thought maybe you could pick up some steaks for Saturday night since it's our last night at the beach. Oh, and don't forget lots of ice. Pete and Roberta are bringing all of their coolers and I told them we'd bring plenty of ice. Can you also get the van checked out tomorrow? It's making a funny noise and I don't want to break down on the trip."

"Anything else?" asks Alex, already mentally rearranging his schedule to get the van into the shop.

"Just your stuff. Are you taking your laptop again this year?" asks Judy, somewhat plaintively.

"I know you hate it, but I've got some big deals in the works and I just can't leave them for a week. Jerry was really riding me today and I just have to do this. I promise I'll only check it once or twice a day."

"That's not so bad. It's that darned cell phone going off all the time. I guess that's coming, too?" Judy asks.

"Yeah, I really can't be out of touch," says Alex. "You know the world will stop spinning if I don't answer a call from one of my customers when they need me," his voice dripping with sarcasm. Alex wishes he could just get away with no ties to the office. "How do people do that for a whole week?" he wonders silently.

"Well, if you have to, you have to," replies Judy. "I'll go call Roberta and let her know we'll be ready to head out Saturday at 7 a.m. Do you think you can help get the kids up and dressed by then?" Judy says as she heads for the kitchen.

Alex barely hears Judy, as he is lost in thought. "Jerry wants me to be back for an important meeting on Friday. Judy is going to explode when she finds out we might have to come back a day early. Jerry has no respect for my time or my family. I'll talk to him again before we leave. I hope I catch him in a good mood."

▶ Paula—The Professional Salesperson

Paula and her husband, Ted, are putting the finishing touches on their vacation plans too. They are headed for Martha's Vineyard for a week with some friends.

"So, are we all ready?" Paula asks as she sits down for dinner.

"All set. I printed the tickets for the flight and checked on the rental car. We got a convertible again. I called the rental office and the cottage will be ready by 2 p.m. for us. I even added a little extra something for us," Ted says with a wink.

"That sounds like heaven. Did you get the tickets for the whale watching?" asks Paula.

"I sure did; we're booked on the Laura Belle with Captain Ernie. And I confirmed the all-day sail on the catamaran. This is going to be great."

"I can't wait. Maybe we can take a little tour of some antique shops while we're there. Or maybe we'll just lounge on the beach and let people bring us cool drinks. What do you think?" Paula inquires.

"I think we'll do whatever we feel like when we get there. We've got 10 whole days to decide what we want to do. Oh by the way, are you bringing your computer and phone this year?" asks Ted, somewhat apprehensively.

"Well, Ron is covering for me at work so I shouldn't need the computer. I told him I'd take the phone but leave it in the room. I'll check it each night but I told him to only call if it was an emergency," replies Paula.

▶ Mark—The Magnetic Salesperson

Mark and Maria are planning a vacation too. This year they are headed to Greece where they are staying at a resort and spa. Each year they choose somewhere special that will be both enjoyable and an educational experience for the kids.

"So, are we all set?" Mark asks at dinner.

"Ready to go. The car is coming to get us Saturday at 8 a.m. We land in Athens at 6:30 p.m. The resort will have a car pick us up at the airport. Then it's two glorious weeks in the Isles!" smiles Maria.

"I'm really looking forward to this," says Mark. "I think the kids will love the two-day sail between the islands. Benny is so excited about sleeping on a boat he can't stand it. And I can't wait to see Athens. All that ancient history. Do you have your spa days planned?" asks Mark with a smirk, knowing the answer.

"You know I do. While you're cruising the Aegean with the kids, I'll be slathered in mud, rubbed and massaged and wrapped in seaweed," Maria sighs.

"Sounds like fun. Sorry I'll miss it," Marks says playfully. He knows how much Maria enjoys her spas and thinks she deserves a few days to herself. She works hard with the kids and her charities. "Are we confirmed with the Montaldos?" asks Mark, mentioning a couple he and Maria met in Italy two years ago.

"Yep, I got an email from Gina yesterday confirming everything. We're meeting them in Mykonos. We'll be there two days. They are bringing Julia and Antonio so the kids can play in the pool while we bask in the sun," says Maria laughing. She knows they have to watch the kids, but it is fun to see them sorting out the English and the Italian with their friends. "Do you have everything at work under control?"

"Sure do. Sylvia is prepared for everything and Linda will handle anything she can't. I'm ready to go as soon as I finish packing. "Hon, thanks for taking care of everything. You're the best." Mark kisses his wife and gives her a hug.

Secret # 6
Average Salespeople **Think Short-Term**
Professional Salespeople **Think Long-Term**
Magnetic Salespeople **Think Life-Long**

▶ Average Salespeople Think Short-Term

Average salespeople's short-term vision negatively impacts both their professional and personal lives. They are stuck in a land of status quo, doing the same things over and over again, whether it is prospecting the same old way or going on the same old vacation year after year.

They take each day as it comes without seeing the bigger picture. They simply cannot see the forest for the trees. They do not make positive adjustments to what they are doing or how they are living, unless they are forced to—often from a fear of loss.

Average salespeople have some general ideas of goals, but lack the commitment and discipline to define and reach them. If they do commit to a goal, they will usually take the easy route to get there. But if the going gets too tough, they retreat to comfortable habits and activities.

In sales, Average salespeople may try focusing on a new market but throw in the towel when they do not get immediate rewards. Their short-term focus is a reflection of their immediate gratification mentality. If the pay off does not come quickly, they can rationalize and justify their old ways of doing things with "I tried that and it really didn't work for me."

Because of his short-range vision, Alex is like most Average salespeople. He gets up every day, gets dressed and heads to work with no real idea of what he wants to accomplish. He has a vague goal of wanting to earn more money, but no real idea of where he wants his life to go. The winging-it approach leads to unpredictable, or predictably low, income, which has kept him stuck in his current house, driving his old car and vacationing at the same place.

▶ Professional Salespeople Think Long-Term

Professional salespeople make their decisions and choose their clients based on a long-term plan, not on next week's paycheck. They have clear goals for all aspects of their lives. These goals are articulated, written and reviewed on a regular basis.

Unlike Average salespeople, Professionals have figured out that they have to look at the long-term implications of their actions or lack of action. For example, they will invest in developing referral sources or deepening a client relationship, because they recognize that their actions may lead to more business in the future.

As part of their overall sales plan, Professionals have developed detailed prospecting systems. For example, Paula can tell you accurately that she needs to meet with three people to close a sale and that her average sale is $5,200. She also knows how to implement her plans, making the required number of contacts every week to hit her sales goals.

▶ Magnetic Salespeople Think Life-Long

Magnets understand that building a practice is more than just having a successful career—they are building a way of life. They understand that to be truly successful they must align their work and sales practice with their personal values and desires and vice versa. They take the time to look far into the future and decide where they want to be in 10, 20 or 30 years. Then they develop a plan and set a course to get there.

Rather than simply taking what comes to them, Magnetic salespeople proactively work toward their life goals, crafting and refining their strategies along the way. They understand that their vacations, hobbies, family time and everything else of importance to them will be impacted by the way they set up their professional lives. Consequently, they carefully design a life that will give them all the rewards they desire in a balanced and meaningful way.

Magnets create successful marketing plans and strategies to attract the kind of business they want.

Because they are experts, they look for ways to further develop and capitalize on their expertise.

Consequently, Magnetic salespeople are willing to invest in themselves and their careers. They have learned that if they put forth the time, effort and resources to improve, they will reap the rewards. Magnets are known to invest 10% of their income back into their own personal and professional development. That way, they can continue to bank on their future.

Summary

To become more Magnetic, you should:

- **Determine your personal vision.**

- **Align your professional and personal goals with your vision and values.**

- **Focus on creating life balance without making unwanted sacrifices.**

- **Invest 10% of your income back into personal and professional development.**

(A P P E N D I X)

Additional Information

▶ Acknowledgements

There are many people who have inspired and guided us in the writing and publishing of this book. Special thanks to Tim Moore of Dancing Elephants Achievement Group; Linda Barrett of All the Buzz; Linda Ruth and Derrick Ruth of AlphaGraphics at the Shoppes at Bellgrade; Cristina Del Bueno and Jennifer Yeager of Right Angle Consulting; Joyce Davis of Square One Creative, L.L.C.; Mark Ishman of Stark Law Group, P.L.L.C.; and Yvonne Kimler. Each played a hand in supporting us in our efforts. Speaking of hands, we appreciate Gus Iurillo of the Entrepreneur Source for his—one of them is on the cover of this book thanks to the wonderful photography of Lee Brauer of Lee Brauer Photography.

▶ About The Authors

Will Turner and Laura Posey are the founders of Dancing Elephants Achievement Group. Both have extensive sales, sales management and sales training experience. Over the years, they have read or participated in many of the more popular sales training programs in the market and realized that most of what salespeople are taught is outdated or ineffective.

Consequently, they developed the Sales Magnetism program that has been embraced by salespeople and small business owners nationwide. Their clients increase sales 56% on average in the first year of participating in this program. In addition to improved sales results, their program participants express relief and gratitude to have a sales approach that is based on principles of integrity, truth and common sense.

More About Will Turner:

Will is the President of Dancing Elephants Achievement Group. He has worked in marketing and sales for the past twenty years. Will admits to having been a very reluctant salesperson for many years early in his career before he realized you do not have to act like a typical salesperson to be a great salesperson.

Will transitioned a long career in sales and sales management into his current role at Dancing Elephants. In addition to training and presenting, Will is the author of *Impact!*, a monthly e-newsletter on sales performance.

Will lives in Bellevue, an older tree-lined neighborhood in Richmond, Virginia. He enjoys spending time with his teenage daughter, Crandall, even though she describes him as a dork. Despite battered knees, doctor warnings and racing mishaps, he remains an addicted marathoner and triathlete. When he is not abusing his body in the name of health and fitness, he relaxes by oil painting.

Will is a graduate of Virginia Tech and has a MBA from Virginia Commonwealth University.

More About Laura Posey:

Laura brings much passion to her work as Vice President and Co-Founder of Dancing Elephants Achievement Group. She is a "firecracker" who likes to create and get things done. Over the years, she has received numerous awards and recognition for her sales and management contributions to different organizations. Laura's extensive sales career has covered the gamut, from insurance to cars. She broke into sales in high school by selling cutlery door-to-door.

Laura is a self-described golf-nut. She is obsessed with breaking 80. She also is crazy about dogs. Gracie, her Ibizan hound, has Laura wrapped around her paw and Gracie knows it! Laura loves to travel as well. She has trekked across most of the U.S. and enjoys traveling in Europe. She even put down roots in Germany for a couple of years to study, work and immerse herself in a different culture.

Laura is a Summa Cum Laude graduate of State University of New York (SUNY at Buffalo), and is currently completing her MBA at Virginia Commonwealth University.

▶ Other Resources From Dancing Elephants Achievement Group

Will Turner and Laura Posey, along with other seasoned Sales Magnets at Dancing Elephants, speak to conventions and organizations and can customize a presentation for your group. They also have their messages on a variety of audio programs.

In addition, Dancing Elephants Achievement Group offers ongoing sales training programs, classes and workshops. These include:

- **Six Secrets of Sales Magnets**
  Six-Week Teleclass

- **Mastering Sales Magnetism**
  12-Month Program

- **Mastering Sales Magnetism for Business Owners**
  12-Month Program

For more information, contact:

Dancing Elephants Achievement Group
2100 B Maywill Street
Richmond, VA 23230
804-254-4122
FAX 804-254-2711

www.dancingelephants.net

Receive FREE articles on improving your sales and becoming a SALES MAGNET.

Each month, **Dancing Elephants Achievement Group** sends out an e-newsletter, *Impact!* It includes sales-related articles designed to help you in your personal and professional development. Read them for insight, inspiration and instruction on how you can be more successful in your sales career.

To receive your FREE subscription to *Impact!*, register on-line at

www.dancingelephants.net.

Here's what some of our subscribers have said:

"This is by far the best e-newsletter I receive. I look forward to every issue."

"The content is always thought-provoking and right on the money. Keep up the good work."

"This is the only newsletter that I read completely. I'd be crazy not to."